Shamanic Dreaming

"Carol never fails to delight with her creative and visionary approach. This book had me smiling all the way through as she expertly guides us along a fun, empowering, and expansive journey toward wholeness and truth within a carefully crafted structure. Her writing and encouragement reflects the depth of her experience, respect, and love for both the mythical and the human. Carol is listening to a wider calling, and with this book as our guide we can't help but do the same."

~ **FAY JOHNSTONE,** shamanic herbalist, Reiki teacher, and author of *Plant Spirit Reiki* and *Plants That Speak, Souls That Sing*

"What do unborn babies dream, floating in their private (yet cosmic) ocean in the womb? Is our umbilical cord a bridge for dreams as well as nourishment? Does our dreaming add to the dreaming of the Earth long before we even see daylight? This new book by Carol Day will help you open doors to the visionary realm, as is your birthright. It will make you an intentional Earth Whisperer, using dreaming as a power tool. You will learn how to continuously place yourself and your relations (plant, animal, mineral, ancestral) in sacred wholeness—the same divine wholeness that dreamed you into being, long before you were even conceived! Treat yourself to this most magical book to become a world-class dreamer!"

~ **IMELDA ALMQVIST,** painter, forest witch, and author of *North Sea Water in My Veins* and *Medicine of the Imagination*

"*Shamanic Dreaming* is full of practical wisdom to find your sense of belonging through time and your continuing role in the unfolding story of the earth. It is full of fun and imaginative ways to connect deeply with yourself and to co-create a better understanding of your calling and the vision for the earth. All this is guided with the support of deep listening to nature, spirit, and the mythical through all dimensions of time and space. This book will change your life—as it did mine! It will give you a sense of living in deep harmony with yourself and the earth in your own unique way. The deep truth and authenticity of this book is so needed for the creation of a new vision for connected earth community."

~ **GILLIAN DUNCAN,** mindfulness coach and
teacher and founder of the Moment Is Now

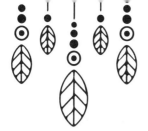

Shamanic Dreaming

Connecting with
Your Inner Visionary

Carol Day

FINDHORN PRESS

Findhorn Press
One Park Street
Rochester, Vermont 05767
www.findhornpress.com

Text stock is SFI certified

Findhorn Press is a division of Inner Traditions International

Disclaimer
The information in this book is given in good faith and intended for information
only. Neither author nor publisher can be held liable by any person for any loss
or damage whatsoever which may arise from the use of this book or any of the
information therein.

Cataloging-in-Publication data for this title is available from the Library of Congress

ISBN 978-1-64411-703-3 (print)
ISBN 978-1-64411-704-0 (ebook)

Printed and bound in the United States by Lake Book Manufacturing, LLC
The text stock is SFI certified. The Sustainable Forestry Initiative® program
promotes sustainable forest management.

10 9 8 7 6 5 4 3 2 1

Edited by Jacqui Lewis
Illustrations by Carol Day
Text design and layout by Anna-Kristina Larsson
This book was typeset in Garamond, Cochin and Cantique

To send correspondence to the author of this book, mail a first-class letter
to the author c/o Inner Traditions • Bear & Company, One Park Street,
Rochester, VT 05767, USA and we will forward the communication,
or contact the author directly at **www.creativeearthensemble.com**.

For all the children of life's longing for itself

(thank you, Kahlil Gibran)

The tribe often thinks the visionary has turned their back on them.
When, in fact, the visionary has simply turned their face to the future.

– Ray A. Davis

Contents

Foreword *by Sandra Ingerman*   9

Preface   11

Introduction   17

Act 1
Calling

Scene 1 Heeding the Calling   20

Chapter 1 Presence and the Three Pillars   21

Chapter 2 Calling   27

Scene 2 Tuning   28

Chapter 3 The Visionary Quest   31

Chapter 4 Dimensions   35

Chapter 5 Passion, Creativity, and Fire   38

Chapter 6 Guides   42

Scene 3 Nature's Communications   45

Chapter 7 Weather Spirits   53

Chapter 8 Birds   62

Chapter 9 Trees   65

Chapter 10 The Fae   68

Scene 4 Animals and Archetypal Support Systems   72

Chapter 11 Brain Opening and Mapping   77

Chapter 12 Dreamtime   81

Chapter 13 Journeying   83

Chapter 14 Archetypes on the Land   86

Scene 5 Reflecting   93

Act 2
Loop

Scene 1 Prep Aligning with Loop   96

Scene 2 Present Lifetime   112

Chapter 1 Land and Perspectives on Time   114

Chapter 2 Rose and Soul   120

Chapter 3 Spirit of the Age   125

Chapter 4 Nature's Eternal Knowing   131

Scene 3 Ancestral Pathways   138

Chapter 5 Introduction to Ancestors   140

Chapter 6 Safe Practice   146

Chapter 7 Dreaming with the Ancestors   153

Chapter 8 Ceremonies of Release and Surrender with the Ancestors   157

Scene 4 Future Pathways   161

Chapter 9 Waters of the Earth   164

Chapter 10 A Cleaning-Up Job   169

Chapter 11 Journeying and the Oracle   174

Chapter 12 Unity   177

Scene 5 Wishes for the Future   182

Finale Vision Hoop   183

Overview of Exercises   188

Bibliography   189

Acknowledgements   190

About the Author   191

Foreword

I was so excited when Carol Day contacted me and told me she had written *Shamanic Dreaming,* a most brilliant book. As civilizations have had to do throughout time, the human race is now at a precipice where we are being asked to let go of the need for individuality and come together as a community of healers, dreamers, and visionaries to support each other and to shift the course of human consciousness.

A crucial area we must focus on is how we can leave a better world to our descendants instead of just expecting them to clean up all the damage we have done, making survival in the future more difficult.

Carol Day is a brilliant visionary herself. One morning she awoke to the words being spoken that visionaries are needed in these times to take care of "the future life map". From these words, this book and practice were born. Reading the book, you will find that one of the core teachings of Carol's work is based on community being able to include as well as listen with honour, respect, and kindness to each member of the Earth community and all that lies beyond. Carol believes that it is with this approach that we can return to a state of harmony and a more connected way of being.

Due to the initiation our planet is going through, people are feeling called to find others with a similar vision so they can feel more support and not feel so alone to deal with all that comes up in such turbulent times. Finding a strong and supportive community is a way to journey into the eye of a storm, where there is silence and peace, to gather one's sense of intuition and innate knowing to return to a place of harmony.

Carol advocates that if we equip everyone with confidence and with practices and encouragement then perhaps we can shift the path we are on now to a positive collective vision. *Shamanic Dreaming* gifts us an entrance into a mystical way of living, helping us to reconnect with the Earth and with the web of life. It opens us to the understanding that we are all actors within a wider mythical theatre where we have the potential to take on new roles. In this place, we can become everyday co-creators of a new story waiting to be born. Carol provides a wealth of tools and practices to enable these roles to be found and to shift our thinking to ways to prosper.

Shamanic Dreaming will really call to those of you who want to step into the role of the visionary and consider what this means for our planet in these times. It is a book that teaches us how to create a beautiful and deep relationship with nature—especially plants, trees, and the weather spirits—and also with the spirit worlds and animal archetypes. An important focus of this book is how to step out of isolation. Its pages teach us how to connect with ancestors—those who live now and the future ones—and how to appreciate the possibilities and importance of connecting and co-creating through this ever-present supportive caravan through time.

Creatively staged as a play, in Act 1: Calling, the curtain opens to the Earth community. The animals, plants, elementals, and spiritual realms behind this act are encountered through working with a visionary model. In Act 2: Loop, systemic constellation and visionary techniques are brought in that take the conversation out into the world and through time. There is also a third Act! This is the Act when you step out of these pages and into your lived life, resonating now with a deeper aspect of the play of life. I imagine that the reader will be able to leave behind any feelings of isolation and realize how much connection they have and that life will continue.

Carol shares illuminating personal stories as well as her gifts of expertise, clarity, love, and compassion to make this an exciting read, while remaining a practical journey. The end result is magnificent as the reader can feel the birth of their own unique vision, supported by the visions of the wide and extensive troupe of performers encountered through this journey.

I have known Carol Day for more than ten years. She is truly a remarkable person. She lives what she teaches and is balanced in her spiritual work as well as the practical side of life. Carol is grounded and so connected to nature. And she teaches from a place of kindness and compassion.

Many years ago, as I was leading a two-year teacher training in Scotland, I developed a health issue partway through. I asked Carol to join our group and assist me in teaching. That is how much faith I have in Carol.

Carol is a true visionary, and she used her creative brilliance to bring us this book, *Shamanic Dreaming*, to help create a healthy community. This book is a gem and so important for our times.

– **Sandra Ingerman, MA,** world-renowned shamanic teacher
and award-winning author of 12 books including
Walking in Light and *The Book of Ceremony*

Preface

It took a while to figure out a name for this book. This book is born of a shimmering knowledge that if we find a way to include everyone and everything then somehow we can slip back into a version of wholeness that is sonorous and true. Over the last two years, the ideas on these pages have been crystallizing. It was originally through client work that I found myself beginning to tap into a way of working with individuals and groups inspired by wondering, "how can we find a way to listen better and create templates that bring in the exact type of listening that is needed?" Something felt missing in the way I was conditioned to hold space. I felt if we could do this then perhaps people and systems could relax in relief. In my work as an artist, writer, visionary, counsellor, nature educator and constellation therapist (I know—I need to find a title that includes all of these together!) I am used to working with the imaginary realms and to holding space within nature and multi-realmed environments. I was feeling a strong desire to demote the human in me from her strange ivory tower of thinking she knows best and try to invent a framework for exploration that would hand over the listening act to a wider and more effective community.

As with everything I seem to do, listening to a desire took me to the creation of a framework. In this book, Act 1: Calling stumbled out of my fingers through the keyboard with the clear message that this work was to help people engage with a wider calling in nature and the animal archetypal realms. I tried out the content as a three-month course. It appeared to work well. I thought I was done and I would put the material with some other words to a publisher. However, the ancestors and future ones had different ideas. In the dreamtime, they came knocking at my door, speaking of the importance of opening up consciousness to their continuous connection with us here in the present. It became clear I was to create Act 2: Loop and that the animals, plants, ancestors and future ones were to be included in this project too. I tried out Loop with some people. It seemed that the two pieces of work joined together as a kind of gyroscope. A design was clicking into place. What I am finding has landed in me more than anything is that vision has a consciousness of its own. There is a visionary field out there that works through all times and realms and if we can settle into that and be a safe listening model, much power for creation and wonder is released.

Vision calls. It really does. It calls to and from a wider continuum.

Vision calls all the way through this book! So the title *Shamanic Dreaming* came into being. *Shamanic Dreaming* is a fun project that helps us to open up to a wider continuum. It is also a joyful rendezvous with circle consciousness!

Many hours of my life have been spent thinking about continuums and circles. I have no idea why the circle should fascinate me so much, although in the fairy story of everything, perhaps the clue is in what I was "called", because I was given the name Carol at birth and a carol is "a round" or a circle dance. Significantly, the only toy I still have from my childhood is a hula-hoop from when I was aged around seven. Everything else went to the charity shop as soon as I left home, but the green circle that I would spend hours twirling at my waist remained.

What interests me about circles is the eternal pull in them. They make me think about what keeps this great show of life moving and on the road. They also speak of cycles of destiny and a feeling of being in something together. Being human can feel quite lonely at times. Circles have a force that keeps us spiralling and keeps us unquestionably together inside something quite mysterious that speaks of the beyond. Christiaan Huygens, the famous Dutch mathematician, astronomer and physicist, called this phenomenon of circling the "centripetal force".[1] Back in the 1980s in high school physics lessons, I would sit contemplating this force; pondering on the eternal pull of creation that is intrinsically held in the cyclical nature of our solar system, in the wider galaxies of which we are a part, and in ourselves. To this day, I constantly wonder at how we live inside the spell of day and night as our planet twirls around to face the sun and then turn away from it. Each day, we behold the dependability of the gentle companionship of the phases of the moon as it orbits our Earth. What an incredible orchestra of spins and cycles this experience of life is; all pulled onwards by the force of a vision that is somehow always ahead of us. In actuality it is just there because of the hoop of the circle and its inevitable turning and it is a turning that perhaps is destined to never stop. Vision will perpetually call us on.

---

1   C. Huygens, *De Vi Centrifuga, Oeuvres Complètes de Christiaan Huygens* XVI (Leiden: University Library, 1659) pp. 255–301 HUG 10, f.87r.

I have been listening to this calling for ever. From the pulsing of a mother's blood through the circulating systems from and to her heart to the less audible but noticeable calling of the outside world that we are all born into, the listening to what is calling endures. This cycling and response to a greater cycling is the backdrop to an internal process that mirrors it. "What did I do yesterday?" "What am I doing now?" "Where will I be tomorrow?" come my thoughts. I am referring to this time cycle all the time, oscillating to find balance and sanity. The past feeds me and the future gives me something to get excited about. The present is holding me and attaching me to a base. Without that I couldn't survive.

In my story, something happened when I was twenty-eight years old to detach me from the dependability of life's hoops. Somehow, when my grandmother died, I couldn't properly get back into rhythm with everything again. After that, a long journey of an exploration of cycles, balance and connection was necessitated that happened from the inside out. It has taken me what feels like aeons to get back in sync, but on the way to reconnect, I have learnt so much about the many realms and planes beyond the simple flow, and the importance of always considering the whole as a part of this journey. The journey also took me into creating visionary models to help others to connect with a wider appreciation of the members of this show of life. I was inspired to build structures that could support and re-educate consideration and inclusion. "Calling" and "Loop", the two Acts within this book, will convey this all to you. The two Acts of this book are ready to slip you into the worlds of the calling vision!

Shamanic Dreaming is an entrance to a mythical way of living that can help to empower and reconnect a race of humans with their Earth and the web of life. When we all open up to the idea that we are partaking in a modern-day myth and take steps to key in with the greater theatre of which we are a part, a race of everyday co-creators of a new story can be born. Can we take the steps to listen to the longing we are each all experiencing within ourselves right now and match this with a wider calling held in the fabric of everything?

The year in which I write this book has been a year of a shake- up of our guiding systems. It has been a year of exposing the limits of these systems. We find ourselves at a crossroads, with the choice to turn inwards and find an intuitively accessed truth. The chance to bring authority back to the senses of each individual and find a new collective meeting ground through mutual access to an inner vision is here. If we can provide stations that equip all of us people with the confidence, practices and encouragement to tune in, then perhaps we can change the future with a collective vision. These are the hopes of this book!

The book works with a visionary formula. I developed this simple recipe over years of helping people to find their own ways in a world that has so much more to it than, as Hamlet says, can ever be "dreamt of in your philosophy". I have long been working with the notion that the books of these times are not just for reading, but are for action. In the course of this book, you will find yourself being led through activity-promoting chapters where you will be guided to connect with the nature worlds and realms beyond this one. I believe that the combined reading and living of a book enables the task of releasing each of us to realize our part in a mythical life. You will find yourself communicating in a way that includes not only the everyday humans we are encouraged to connect with on a daily basis, but also the local community as a realm of nature-filled interchanges and chances to open to an extended field of interconnection. *Shamanic Dreaming* can be a kaleidoscopic experience of a rich and lively hub of inspiring principles for you. As it takes place in two acts, my intention is that you and your life can be the third Act!

It was one sunny afternoon in 2015, when a buffalo wandered into my meditation and dropped a yellow circle onto my lap that the concept was seeded. Buffalo conveyed clearly a calling to help create community with the Earth again. She asked me to open myself to visualize everything that could possibly be to belong within this yellow hoop. Since then, I have been following the search and deepening my connection with the calling of the land, its communities—animal, mineral, vegetable and beyond— and the realms behind this one, asking for a model that can be taken into people's lives to help bring this vision alive again.

Through the material on these pages, the calling that is within both the self and within everything is brought into stark consciousness. The shift of focus from the "I" we customarily live by to the collective "we" alludes to a quantum ethos. Focus on the "I" in our language and positioning of "self" can mean that we are out of sync with our wider nature and miss out on a lot. A particle becomes fixed once observed and registered, yet it is only there because it is part of a greater wave. I have written a book that helps us to come out of the particle to find our place within a much bigger and more wondrous wave. The truth is that this wave is going on all of the time and everything is naturally interacting with it! Turning the pages of

Act 1: Calling will take you on a journey feeling into why on Earth you are here, what on Earth is going on and what it is that can open up for us and be possible when we feel ourselves as a part of a much bigger orchestra.

Act 2: Loop is written as a time travel adventure through the present, past and future lands. After picking up the calling in these times, Loop then travels into the past to meet the longing of the ones who came before us. The vision and experiences of the ancestors are appreciated in relationship to what we experience today. Working with nature portals on the land and the practice of attuning with some of the nature and animal guides, we visit the place of the past to relieve pressure and allow a flow. Finally, visiting the future ones, we understand the importance of what we hold today in creating the environments and conditions for the future. In this visit we find confirmation and hope for continuance.

The book concludes with a ceremony. Through the making of a vision hoop, a dynamic act of power and creativity is forged that helps to set the way for you and wield the vision that is both our own and that of the planet in these times.

I look forward to joining you out of the unrest in the collective Act 3 that goes beyond this book and which is the lived zest and spirit of the great adventure that calls us all!

Carol Day
Arcadia, Scotland

Introduction

Welcome to *Shamanic Dreaming*—a visionary quest and adventure inside your very own life! The curtains are about to open! This book may be read in one sitting, to then return to the tasks as time affords, or you may read and partake in its actions in manageable chunks over a few months. Although I recommend following the timeline of its pages, it might be that you have different sections that stir you at different times. Please go with your own knowing.

The book is written in two Acts like a play. I invite you to feel your life as a story inside which you can be an empowered player. The play you enter holds the intention of empowering you to be a co-playwright in this immense theatre that is our Planet Earth.

This visionary process outlined in this book is designed to connect you even more deeply with the calling you hold within. By opening you to the nature world and the seasons turning, a movement alongside the calling of the Earth and everything can be reached.

You will find yourself coached by nature and presence and will be helped to understand, clear and transform difficulties in connection with what is calling you in this lifetime. A new and expanded way of mapping yourself and feeling connection with the Earth community, what goes beyond this, past, present and future can all come into play.

The structure of this book is essentially two Acts of ten scenes in total with a finale piece. You will find the scenes play as chords of expression and times that will tune you too!

You will encounter Earth Whisperer tasks to set the material in action and sections for taking notes to remember what you experience along the way. I recommend you equip yourself with the following before you begin:

- a notebook;
- pens and coloured pencils;
- a sketchbook;
- pastels and paints;
- a camera;

- a voice-recording device;
- headphones;
- outdoor clothing (waterproofs, walking boots, hat, gloves, scarf according to seasons—this is a book for all weathers!);
- a frame drum and beater or tambourine;
- a rattle;
- a resource of drumming tracks and soothing music;
- tree identification book.

Act 1

Calling

^ ⌄ ^

Act 1 will commence shortly!

Are you ready to open up the dimensions and bring
your inner calling to the fore? Here we begin an Act of potential
and focus, so please prepare for potential great openings!
So, we begin! Into a play about calling we step.

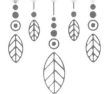

Scene 1: Heeding the Calling

Vision and Visionary

The word "vision" refers to the faculty or state of being able to see. The word "vision" can also be used to define the ability to think about or plan the future with imagination or wisdom. Someone who works in this way is known as a visionary. A few years ago, I started to use the word "visionary" to define the practice I was developing when I received a strong message in a dream that what the world needs in these times is mythically oriented people who can hold a strong and inclusive vision for the future. Visionary feels apt to describe a future-looking way that can be most beneficial for our planet. As an artist and writer, I also love and value the power of imagination and creativity. Visioning has a lot of imagination and creativity wrapped up in it too!

The Triangle of Knowing, Nature, and Trust

Over the years of developing a practice that helps vision to open in people, I have created a formula. This can be applied to help us to enter a space where connection, embodied practice and open-mindedness can all be achieved. The formula holds the circle as its symbol with a triangle within this and then a dot in the centre. The centre is presence, the three corners of the triangle are knowing, nature and trust and the circle is what I call the wholeness template. The gaze of wholeness surrounding everything is important with this work because it allows what goes beyond the story to come in and hold space. This opens up the possibility for healing and flow that goes beyond what we could ordinarily imagine. The wholeness template represents a place for everything that goes on beyond the constraints of what we are led to believe is the "everyday world". I believe that coming back to an investment to place ourselves in wholeness is the key to entering the mythical framework that I speak of in the preface. I call the formula "Presence and the Three Pillars".

Chapter 1

Presence and the Three Pillars

Presence is the central pole of the entire visionary practice. It is what runs through everything. It is the act of being present and of not running away or rushing. Presence is when we can unconditionally, while holding awareness and compassion, be able to be present with what is. I see presence as a place of power and courage. It is a stance that takes us out of dialogue and duality and takes us into a space of observation. It allows a meeting with the heart of any matter. Presence is the land where the visionary hangs out. It is a land free of judgement, advice or overlay. My personal feeling of when I get to this place of being able to be present is like the air conditioning comes on. It feels cool and disentangled but also very kind and loving.

With presence as the central pole, the three pillars sit as a triangle of what I refer to as concepts.

A concept is a central principle or idea. It is where conception happens. You can see how this leads us to an original impulse. We are looking to allow the original powerful impulse to come through in visionary work, so engaging with concepts is a good way to build a means for this to happen.

The Three Pillars

Pillar "Nature"

Nature can be likened to essence. It is the inherent qualities or character of anything. Nature is the first pillar of the visionary model. I use the term "innate nature" to suggest that we have an inherent way of being that is akin to nature. Nothing in nature pretends to be anything else (unless it is meant to, as camouflage for survival). The members of the nature world who do change form do so for a specially programmed and consistent reason. Humans, on the other hand, are shape-shifters extraordinaire. We can merge, absorb, project, take on and consume power and identity. We have such a gift, but sadly we have mainly forgotten to set a way to use this gift wisely. Those who do use it often do so—unconsciously—for power-mongering means. This means that our innate nature can be covered up. The skills in shape-shifting are truthfully the tools of the visionary practice. We will be working through becoming more conscious of these skills and releasing what has been taken on or acted out as cover-ups to better reveal our own true or innate natures. This will happen through visiting and immersing ourselves in the concepts.

Pillar "Knowing"

Knowing is connected with having knowledge or awareness about something. It is a word that is often used when something is known that is hidden to many. One of the skills of the visionary is having this rare knowing. (Although I do believe, personally, it can be developed in anyone given the right circumstances.) This is the second pillar.

Pillar "Trust"

Trust is a firm belief in reliability or truth. It is the third pillar. The development of discernment to be able to operate from this place of trust is key to the visionary's ability to operate.

Meeting the Pillars

Nature

Where did nature begin? One of my most mind-opening things to do is to remember that I have been here since the beginning of time. If I hadn't been then I wouldn't be able to feature as I am now. I own my place at the beginnings of life and the great darkness, light, formation of atoms and everything. Read this Big Bang theory as one of the versions of the beginnings of creation:

The "cosmos" begins expanding in the split of a second and in this time turns "nothing" into something the size of an orange. In three minutes the universe has heated into being—a hot soup of electrons, quarks and other molecules. Then follows a long cooling period and with this cooling down, quarks can turn into protons and neutrons. The universe becomes a very hot fog.

Three hundred thousand years later, electrons will combine with protons and neutrons and form atoms (mostly hydrogen and helium). Light can shine. After a billion years from source, things really cool down and hydrogen and helium gases coalesce to become galaxies. Smaller clumps of gas coalesce to become the first stars. After fifteen billion years of galaxies gathering together, the first stars die and throw heavy elements into space. These eventually form into new stars and planets.

The universe is fifteen to twenty billion years old. The Earth is five to six billion years of age.

How beautiful is all that! Our heritage is a deep foundation of spaciousness, temperature, birthing and discovery. Our history as the elements is a long, passionate, powerful, patient, devoted, alchemical and mysterious affair!

Being Concept Nature

Let's meet Nature as the first of the three pillars.

See if you can find a special place in nature with a tree, where you can sit regularly through the next months. It might be your garden or a tree on a walk close to you. Attune to where this place is going to be and resolve to dedicatedly visit this place for the duration of working with this book.

Take about twenty minutes or more for this Being Nature task.

Go to your chosen place in nature. Sit with your back to the special tree that you will visit regularly. Take some time to become present. Focus on your breath and simply become mindful to what chatter might be going on inside your head. You don't need to push it out. Presence is about allowing awareness to arise and comes from a different place to the mind chatter.

Let yourself move into your senses. Touch—feel the air on your skin, touch the ground with your fingers and the surface of the tree, grass and nature around you. Smell—breathe in the scents. Taste—taste the air, lick the grass, tree bark, a flower. Hearing—let your ears take in the sounds. Sight—let your eyes light on everything as if seeing for the first time. Let nature join you through your senses.

In this space, bring yourself to an awareness of being present and in the moment. You are looking to become present with nature both within and without. Now imagine this presence as being able to exist throughout all times. Take yourself to the beginnings of everything. Feel the origins. Feel the today. Allow a conversation to happen, moving with presence with your senses and nature through these two stations of presence.

Bring yourself back. How do you feel about nature now? How do you feel about your own true nature and nature around you? Make some notes on how you found this experience.

Knowing

When we think about the visionary or someone who sees or has "the sight" we are really connecting with the ability to know and are describing this as a way of truly seeing. This kind of sight goes beyond the way the eyes see and into the inner vision. It is this knowing and this development of inner vision and the ability to see to the heart of something that is the second of the three pillars in the visionary model.

The drum, and other instruments that make repetitive noises and have a wealth of symbolism and meaning attached to them to connect us with the communication realms, can take us out of the everyday chatter and into a place of knowing.

Particular things happen to our brain waves when we listen to the sounds of a drum or rattle: in the trance state of drumming, brain waves move out of the beta range (between fourteen and twenty-one cycles per second), in which we are attentive and focused on everyday external activities, and into the alpha, theta and sometimes delta ranges.

Alpha waves vibrate at seven to fourteen waves per second and happen when we are in a relaxed, internal-focused state of well-being. Theta waves vibrate at four to seven cycles per second and are the threshold of the sleep dream state. Delta waves are one to four cycles per second. They are deep sleep. The brains of foetuses emit delta waves.

Animals and the electromagnetic waves of the Earth operate in the alpha range. Yogis see the alpha state as the rhythm of nature. Coming out of beta state definitely enhances our connection to nature.

Being Concept Knowing

You will need a drum or rattle for this Being Knowing task.

Pick up your drum or rattle. Visualize a bubble of light around you that holds presence. Set the intention that you are only available here to connect with your knowing. Choose a colour to coat the bubble around you that sets the boundary that this is a clear space for you. You can extend a second bubble to go all around your home and the boundaries of the land around your home, small garden, balcony or terrace and set the same intention. Sit and connect with being present again. You will become more familiar with this feeling the more you practise these concepts of being.

Now focus on your knowing. Think of a time when you have known something. Begin to tap your drum or rattle. Try to do this for about fifteen minutes. Connect with your knowing and let all your attention and the attention of the drumbeat flow to hold awareness for this knowing. Ask yourself, "Where does this knowing come from?" Feel the origins and authenticity of your knowing. Let it strengthen and take its place. Observe what happens for you.

NOTE: If you don't have a drum you can also do this by playing a drumming track instead, but I highly recommend developing your relationship with presence through drumming and having your own drum.

Come back and thank your drum or rattle and the space that held you. Take some notes.

Trust

Trusting ourselves and developing the ability to discern is the third pillar of the visionary model. Often we learn from not having accurate discernment. Lots of people and situations can be our teachers for this. We will be holding presence for the development of this trust while working with the material in this book.

Being Concept Trust

Go back to your place in nature. Move into a place of presence again. Be in your senses. Take some time to land and be with the Earth and the weather. Feel yourself as a part of this wider system. Now open up to feeling the interconnectedness of everything. Become aware of the different systems within the outer nature operating right now. Feel how they work together and the plan that they are a part of. Feel into your trust for this plan.

Now feel all of the systems going on within you and your body, mind, emotions, passions. Feel your organs and your blood flow, the beating of your heart, your lungs breathing, your eyes and the way your thoughts respond to your eyes working. Feel how you connect with the outer world through your lungs and your sight and thoughts, your sense of smell and your emotions.

Move back again to your awareness of the systems in nature outside of you and the plan everything including you is a part of. Feel into your trust for this plan.

Spend about fifteen minutes in this being with trust. Come out of the task and then make some notes on how you found this and any insight you had.

Chapter 2

Calling

So now it is time for you acquaint yourself with your personal calling and to make a place which will store your calling.

When you picked up this book, what was it that you were feeling called to do or experience? In this chapter you will spend some time opening up whatever it is that is your desire.

First of all, take some time to write down your intention. Feel into it. What is important to you? What would you like to feel like or know better when you have completed this book? What is looking for healing or reconnection? How do you feel your calling?

Write this down and make a special board that you can pin your intention to or a box you can place it inside. Now choose some images to surround your intention with. These can be photos of places, people, ancestors, deities or animals that inspire you. If you choose a box, then you can place objects like special stones inside. The idea is that you energize your intention with things that you find powerful and supportive.

Now make a visit to your special tree or nature place you have located. Whisper or speak your intention to connect with your calling and everything that goes with that to your tree. You may also choose to leave something with the tree that represents your calling and place it inside an opening or hang it loosely from one of its branches.

You can write notes about this too.

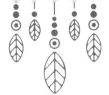

Scene 2: Tuning

The process of tuning begins!

Thirteen years ago, when I first started to write shamanic and visionary courses, my work operated with the title "Restoring Wholeness: the Shaman's Craft". The truth is that restoring wholeness is what any healing project is about. The word healing comes from *hælen,* which means "to become whole". In any restorative work, we are always looking to draw back in what has been rubbed out, suppressed or missed.

I have found that following calling is such a direct, passionate and deep way to draw what is true back in. I think that we are programmed to belong and bring everything back together really! When we attune to the inner calling then the path to restoration can be invigorating and meaningful. Remembering and prioritizing listening to calling as a first step is a revolutionary and powerful act.

In Tuning, we set up the Visionary Quest, mark and plot the territory and find some helpers that we will walk with on our journey.

Earth Tuning

The Earth has always been calling for us to step back into flow with it. The Earth wants us to know ourselves again. As Chief Seattle wrote in his famous letter to President Pierce in 1885, "We are a part of the Earth and it is part of us."[2] Our consciousness resides here. Our cells are made of everything that the Earth provides. It doesn't make sense to see ourselves and the Earth with all its creatures and beings as separate entities. Put this way, we can see that the calling is within each of us. Our part in this show of life right now is to once more find a way to step back into a flow.

Visionary work begins when we open up to vision. This opening up requires making the space, time and personal availability to communicate with the visionary part of our soul. Vision can open when we least expect

---

2 Seattle, and Susan Jeffers, *Brother Eagle, Sister Sky* (New York: Dial Books, 1991).

it but it will find its way through when we make space for it in our lives. Whether we do this through being present, taking time to walk in nature, drawing, writing, drumming or simply by relaxing, a pulse will sound announcing that we are ready for a deeper part of us to open up to let itself be felt. The next part of the process will then be to build a relationship with the deeper part and what communicates with us here. The practice of establishing a connection with the visionary part of our nature is what can be called "attuning".

Attuning to who we are on a level deeper than the everyday thinking and organizational self will bring us into the realm of soul. Unbounded by the definition of form and personality, soul can cross borders and pick up on the communication realm with everything else. This is the way of visionary consciousness. Allowing this attuning to happen is the first step in bringing visionary consciousness back into being. Babies and children attune naturally. Attuning is the way of spontaneous being and play. I wonder what the world would look like if everyone were taught how to stay in touch with and develop this practice of attuning as maturing adults? I am guessing that everything would be able to communicate with everything else again.

The way of the visionary is the practice of the listening one. When we open to listen then we can allow the messages we need to hear to come through.

Today, as part of my writing process, I took myself off on a run to attune to this book and to ask for some signs. It was a few years ago that this work was conceived, when I worked with a manifestation project with the earth element. As mentioned earlier, buffalo came through with a message. The message was that my personal calling was to help bring back a real Earth community by creating work that could support people and the Earth to come back into a flow together again. I have a favourite place on one of my running routes where there is a grove of oak trees and a river. Today as I approached it I found four Highland cattle sitting and standing beneath the oaks: new neighbours on this land. I spent ages standing with them and listening to the deeper message that their presence as buffalo in this realm was bringing to me. This is what I mean by Earth attuning. The Earth is weaving with us all of the time. We just need to be available to hear and see and to be clear about prioritizing listening to our own calling to notice the responses.

Tuning will set you up with material that will support the opening of attuning pathways just like this! It will also support you to develop ways to hold yourself and the calling you personally hold as a priority in your life.

You will just need to read through the **Focus** material in each section. Then you can look to the information in each section for **Setting Up**. This will outline the ideas for the section and support you in moving your vision forwards and in allowing the calling of yourself and the Earth to come through.

The Earth speaks to those who give space to allow a deepening. Together we work to allow and honour this space coming back into place. In Calling we enter into a quest with the Earth and our life. The quest is the "Visionary Quest".

Chapter 3

The Visionary Quest

Focus: Visionary Quest Preparation

We will be beginning a practice of tuning in to the land about and allowing the senses to open by looking at Vision Quests, sacred sites and song lines through different traditions. We set up an Earth Whisperer practice. First, here are some ideas for what can you do each day to begin to make the changes to be ever more available to allow the visionary self to emerge.

1　Be grateful for everything that you encounter, from the water in your shower to the bed that you sleep in, to the neighbour who spoke with you today. This will open appreciation channels that value connection.

2　Live in your senses. Be aware of touch, smell, hearing, sight and taste. This will aid and enhance connection too.

3　Be aware of the spaces between everything. This will help to aerate the pathways.

4　Make a list of the things you are drawn to and like on this earth. This will help you to see what you are already in communion with and what is feeding your soul in some way.

The Earth is attuning too. We are Earth Whisperers, listening to the calling of ourselves and the Earth!

Vision Quests

Vision Quest is a term that was probably first used by nineteenth-century anthropologists to describe the rite-of-passage ceremonies of some indigenous American cultures.

Vision Quests can be both personal and collective events that are guided and witnessed within a community. They often involve the person who is on the quest spending time alone in nature in search of a personal vision that in its turn becomes a vision to support the entire community. A Vision Quest will often accompany an important landmark or life change in someone's life.

What life change are you currently making that has drawn you to this visionary quest?

Sacred Sites

Vision Quests can open us up to the spiritual aspects of a sacred site. Sacred sites are places within the landscape that have a special meaning or significance to the people of the land. This can be historically through time, and it can also be through a personal connection. Hills, rocks, rivers, trees, plains, lakes, and other natural features can be sacred sites. In coastal and sea areas, sacred sites may include features that lie both above and below water. St Michael's Mount and its causeway, in Cornwall, England, is an example of this.

What sites hold a special meaning or significance for you?

Song Lines and Ley Lines

Song lines and ley lines convey their spiritual aspects in vision quests. The Camino, for example in Spain, is an energy line that is walked to induce vision and healing.

Song line is a term that comes from Australian Aboriginal culture. Song lines are long creation story lines that cross the country, which have been walked throughout time. They geographically and mythically connect sacred sites to their places within the stories of the land and Aboriginal culture. They hold knowledge and frequencies that can be walked and sung for healing and for balancing.

Ley line (or ley) is a term that was first coined in 1921 by Alfred Watkins, an antiquarian who lived in Hereford, England.[3] It describes the energy pathways that run through the Earth. Leys run as straight lines and they flow through sacred sites. Often they cross with other leys at these points. The sacred sites can be felt as nodules holding the vibration of these pathways as they cross, and are portals to their information and healing energy.

Working with the energy lines and sacred sites is a way of tapping into the Earth's system. Walking or attuning to these lines can also support an opening to our visionary nature and intensify our ability to open up to worlds beyond the everyday one we consensually agree to occupy.

Setting Up the Earth Whisperer Practice

Bring forward your intention for the course that you have energized. If you haven't already, write it now as an affirmation of what is already happening for you, e.g. "I am . . . I do . . . This is how it is . . ." This way you bring it into the present.

Now you are going to set up your space for your visionary quest to come.

What is written on the following page is an idea of words to read out each day that holds the template of wholeness, aligns you with the vision of the Earth and casts a gaze of support and resourcing for everything that you do. I recommend that you open up space as a daily practice and that you modify the words overleaf to fit with what you might already do or to find a language that feels true for you.

You may also choose to play a flute, shake a rattle or use another instrument that sets up the intention of the space opening without needing to read the words.

---

3 Alfred Watkins, *The Old Straight Track: Its Mounds, Beacons, Moats, Sites and Markstones* (London: Methuen, 1948). https://archive.org/details/b29827553.

⌃ ⌄ ⌃

Earth Whisperer Space Opening

*Today I open up my heart to connect with the land and all of
the special sites, beings and places on this land. I honour the
ancestors of the land here. I honour all the beings, creatures and
manifestations of nature that live here with me. I see the land
and all of its places and beings being able to be felt, heard, seen
and given audience and inclusion again by humans.*

*I open up my body to be able to connect with the true healthy
energy of this amazing Earth I live as a part of. I set the intention
that I can become more and more in alignment with the calling of
the Earth and the true vibrant essence of the whole of this planet.*

*I open up my connection with the vibrant energy in my own
living body. I feel my intent to be able to listen to and understand
the way of my body and its simple needs. I know that by listening
to my body and by accepting its limitations, its knowing and its
boundaries in each moment I serve this life and myself best. I
know that these needs and limitations can change at any time.*

*I connect with the energy of the personal vision I bring to my life
at this moment and bring a space to mind now where I place this
alongside and within the true potential vision of this planet.*

*I acknowledge that in this moment I honour the power in myself
and in everything to effect positive change. I know that in this
moment I am initiating a pathway for flow. I know that the
pathway for flow is set at a gentle but true gauge so that my
family, my Earth community and myself can feel settled and held.*

⌃ ⌄ ⌃

Chapter 4

Dimensions

Focus: Opening Up Dimensions

There are many dimensions. As humans, we live within the scope of what we ordinarily believe we can access as the dimensional axis. These are one-dimensional (a dot connecting a dot); two-dimensional (a plane of existence with two dots and another to give width and height); three-dimensional (volume and space without time) and four-dimensional (space with time and the ability to travel). The visionary part of our nature has a natural inclusion of the many other dimensions. In physics, string theory places this as ten or eleven.[4] The best way to find the truth of this for yourself is to conduct some journeys into all dimensions and find out from your own visionary source!

From a scientific perspective, the fifth dimension is a dimension we open to where we are able to see the higher dimensions. These are imperceptible to us, scientists believe, because they exist on a subatomic level. These dimensions are curled in on themselves in a process known as compactification. The dimensions from here on out really deal with possibilities. In the fifth dimension there would be a new world that would allow us to see the similarities and differences between our world and this new one, existing in the same position and having the same beginning as our planet, i.e., the Big Bang.

The sixth dimension is an entire plane of new worlds that would allow you to see all possible futures, presents and pasts with, again, the same beginning as our universe.

In the seventh dimension up through the ninth, we have the possibility of new universes with new physical forces of nature and different laws of gravity and light. The seventh dimension is the beginning of this, where we

---

4   M. B. Green, J. H. Schwarz and E. Witten, *Superstring Theory* (Cambridge: Cambridge University Press, 1999).

encounter new universes that have a different beginning from ours. That is, they were not born from the Big Bang.

The eighth dimension is a plane of all the possible pasts and futures for each universe, stretching infinitely.

The ninth dimension lays bare all the universal laws of physics and the conditions of each individual universe.

Some scientists believe that the multiverse has only ten dimensions, while others put that number at eleven. However, a universe cannot have more than eleven dimensions according to Novikov's self-consistency theory. Self-consistency is a conjecture that states that it is impossible to create paradoxes by time travel because the past cannot be changed. After ten or eleven dimensions, consistency would become unstable and need to collapse back down into eleven or ten dimensions. At the point of ten or eleven dimensions, anything is possible. There are all futures, all pasts, all beginnings and all ends, infinitely extended, a dimension of anything you can imagine. Everything comes together.

Reading this, you can see how we are all conditioned to have a set expectation and a singular lens perspective. In this week's setting up we will be setting up an honouring of our life in the four-dimensional matrix and grounding ourselves here, and then opening up with safe boundaries to encounter the dimensions that go beyond.

Opening up with safe boundaries is important. You have probably spent most of your life operating at a frequency and with an ego consciousness that keeps you sane and in keeping with the rest of your community and life. We need to keep our belonging with this, while at the same time being able to travel out and then gradually change the mapping and the openness of our culture.

I have found that setting an intention to stay grounded is one of the most secure ways to work with opening. The following two weeks will give you further guidelines for safe practice.

Setting Up the Earth Whisperer Practice

Pick up a drum or a rattle. Imagine a bubble of translucent light all about your aura. Set the intention that you are kept clear and that you are very much in your body and grounded.

Begin by rattling or drumming and feeling your feet and how they touch the Earth. Feel the power of the Earth beneath you. Feel the physical form

Dimension Opening

of the Earth. Feel the physicality of your body. Welcome in the different parts of the physical Earth like the plants, soil and trees and welcome also the different parts of the physical form of you. Feel the blood, skin, hair, organs, flesh and bones.

When you feel grounded and in your physical body on the Earth, move through the ten (or eleven) dimensions in turn and feel them there. You can read the above as you do it the first few times to get an idea of their scale and influence. Over time you will feel them more as you sense them or as they appear to you. See if you can divine a colour or a symbol for each of the dimensions to help you begin to map them.

Set the intention that you are only available to work with opening to the dimensions while being able to return to life very grounded in your body and ask your body in a felt sense to set this as an intention with you. Feel the tree that you have connected with in the first week holding this intention with you and feel into its roots. Know that you can go and sit with your tree to ground at any time you feel you would benefit from taking time to become more in this everyday dimension.

When you feel secure with this, now as you rattle or drum, in your own way, invite the different dimensions of being to operate with you and through you.

Come slowly back into your body and your connection with the Earth. Feel your connection with your everyday senses of smell, touch, sight, hearing and taste. Go out into nature for five minutes or more to really feel yourself here. Take some notes.

Chapter 5

Passion, Creativity, and Fire

Focus: Opening to Passion

What is passion? I think of passion as something that is a bit like a fire inside our being. Could it be the stirring within that makes each of us who we are and guides us towards what attracts us the most? Passion energizes us for sure.

Opening to passion, or responding to the clues that remind us what our passion is, is akin to following our calling.

I often think about the passion of the Earth. There have been times in my life when I have experienced loss or devastation and I want everything to stop frozen in time and listen to my shock with me. Instead, I have been utterly aware of the striking resolve of the Earth to keep on moving forward no matter what. "Time and tide wait for no man," says Chaucer. The Earth's drama to continue and not stop tugs me into a remembrance that I too need to let this grief or agony move, move, move. Through the passion of night following day, the moon spinning the Earth, the seasonal evidence of the Earth orbiting the sun and the relentless flow of the life of those we love and know moving through death, the theatre of the Earth's passion show continues. When I feel the Earth, I feel how passion is the great instigator of this creative vortex of life we live as a part of. It is meeting the passion of that which continues (almost brutally felt sometimes) in nature that in the end has been that which has brought the greatest healing.

The areas of closing down and fear are often what we need to focus on freeing more than anything else in order to let healing happen.

I mentioned the ego in the last section. The ego is what the psychologists Sigmund Freud and Carl Jung brought to the world's attention as a model of that which keeps us safe. As conditioned humans, we respond to the rules and the sensing of the ego as it shows us what we have internally learnt is accepted or is safe. The ego will keep us closing down or it will play tricks with us to help us to avoid something that is going to be painful or have us exiled from our tribe. Often following our calling challenges the ego. This might be exactly why we have never followed it before!

So the job with the ego here, in being able to follow a calling that might challenge its formation, is to bring in what can hold, love no matter what and compassionately listen with discernment to its messages.

This is where bringing in the model of the creativity wheel below can come in handy and the task of accompanying this with opening up the passion lines can be relieving.

In the shamanic "elements" or "medicine" wheel, passion is the element of fire. Fire works as that which gives warmth and light and also as that which brings huge transformational energy. When I work with people and the subject of projects and passion, I am always noticing how when the passion comes in it also involves the burning through of a previous idea of self.

Transformation is an energetic process.

Creativity is a full cycle. Below is a map of the creativity wheel that marks the seasons and the elements as part of its course. You can see how spring moves through to winter and that the process of death and picking up what is behind the veil is as much a part of creativity as the visible process of life in our world. Following the calling and the messages of our passion will necessitate including the burning and the letting-go part of the process of transformation.

Be aware of what is let go of or what has to move out of the way as you step more into opening up to connection and expansion. Try to let the people around you know in advance that there will be some changes so that you can be ready to work together through them.

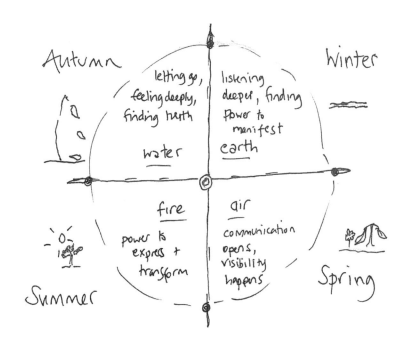

Creativity Wheel

Setting Up the Earth Whisperer Practice

Have a look at the creativity wheel above. What do you notice as you view it? What stands out for you? Notice what feels weak or strong for you.

Find five stones and place them in a circle at a distance of about two feet from each other so that they can be the four directions of the compass and the centre. Place the stones as East as Air, South as Fire, West as Water and North as Earth elements. Take your rattle and move to stand with the centre stone and feel a ring of light around you where the compass points move through. Acknowledge that your body and this Earth exist with the intelligent energy and cooperation of each these elements. Now whistle and rattle to call in each direction. You are opening up a relationship with and acknowledging the presence and utter importance of the four elements in your life. Now feel yourself in the centre and whistle and rattle to acknowledge all of the different dimensions that operate that you opened up a connection to last week. Notice how you sense this in your body and how you perceive this in your circle.

Step out of the wheel and notice how you feel now.

⌃ ⌄ ⌃

This week, take time to go for a walk to open up the passion lines. Simply open the creativity wheel as above and then with your connection to your passion open, move outside and see where you are led. You might go to your tree, or you might be called to jump on a bus or into your car to go and visit a special place. See what calls you. But know that with the intention of opening up the passion lines, something can happen that is important.

If you can try to set yourself a passion walk with the Earth every week from now on, this will act as a way of connecting your passion even more with the passion and communication systems of the Earth.

After your visit, take time to write or create something that can map your journey or allow the passion line to flow into a creative act. As much as possible match this with the intention you made for this book!

Chapter 6

Guides

Focus: Working with a Tuning Guide

Put simply, a guide is something or someone that we can make a clear connection with and that can guide us as we move between our notion of the everyday and that which goes beyond. A guide is able to bridge the dimensions for us to take us safely into the visionary parts of our nature and back into everyday reality again. I often feel the guide as being a part of me, but a part with which I need to have a relationship so that I can filter into a different space and time and open up communication from my everyday ego level.

In this section you will be finding a tuning guide to work with. Opening up to the visionary realm requires that we all hold clear boundaries. Overwhelm can happen otherwise. We work with the tuning guide and also set up a practice with a grounding guide. This supports you to be able to keep your feet on the ground! I call this guide a Protector.

The people I see working most effectively as visionaries are those who have a clear and simple aim. The people who I see going round in circles are those who don't keep focus or who open availability to that which goes beyond their remit. You need to really state what you are and are not

available for to be what I call a "director of flow" with visionary work. To support effectiveness, you will be guided to work with a model of a contract (see below). Please adjust the wording to suit your own needs.

Often guides appear through nature and also come to us at particular stages in our lives. Trees and birds can be guides and signs, for example. Your tuning guide will be a guide that steps forward to help you to tune in to what is the right way for you. I call this guide the Pathfinder.

Setting Up the Earth Whisperer Practice

1 Take your calling intention for a walk out in nature and ask for a guide from nature to come to you. Chances are they have already appeared for you at some stage before! See who comes!

2 Pick up your drum or rattle. You are going to open up to the Pathfinder guide. Drum or rattle with your intention for Act 1: Calling in mind. Ask to be taken to the tree you use for your base for this work (you may also choose to go there in person and make this journey out in nature). Ask the tree to appear for you or speak to you as a tree guide. Now ask to be taken to meet a Pathfinder guide for this course. When you find them ask them lots of questions and ask them why they have come to you. Simply being with the guide can be a way of intuitively accessing lots of information.

3 Pick up your drum or rattle. Ask the tree guide now to take you to meet a Protector who will act as a grounding guide for you. When you have established a connection with this guide (it could be a colour, a rock, an animal, a plant, for example) ask the guide why it is a Protector for you and how to work with it. Talk to the Protector about the contract you are going to set. You can also do this as a written piece of work. There are some ideas for this below. Know that you can choose to call in this guide and "wear" it about you like a cloak at any time to help you to ground or to block out any toxic energy in different environments.

Contract for Practice

Think of what you are and are not available for and set boundaries. I suggest the following as a model to begin with.

I am available for:

I am only available to connect with that which supports my Calling that I hold for this book. I am only available to connect with that which is true and healing. Anything else that is attracted to my light or intention is taken by guides and healing spirits that surround my home to places on the Earth's surface that bring the healing they need. I don't even need to be aware of any of this happening.

To anyone who sees my light and feels the pull to engage that isn't working in a supportive way for me, I now see my aura carrying the message, "You can access this in you too" and the sign "Closed". Thank you to these guides and to the power of contract and direction.

I am not available for:

I am not available for any healing projects or for taking on anything for any other persons. My Protector guide keeps me shielded and true.

︿ ﹀ ︿

When you are out and about these next couple of weeks in particular, why not play at being a bit of a sleuth working with these guides!

Call in your Pathfinder guide and internally connect with them for guidance and to start to operate with more discernment about what your course of action is according to the intention you hold. Try to journey to them weekly if you can.

Connect with your Protector at regular points. You will possibly begin to notice the quality of the energy about you more easily. You can ask yourself what you are guided to do to support the energy in your environments to be more positive and supportive for you.

Notice your nature guides and when they turn up for you.

Your groundwork with Tuning is complete and ready to lead you into the realms of nature and the animal archetypes. You will find the next two scenes less intensive and more flowing with your intention visionary quest style.

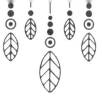

Scene 3: Nature's Communications

Your work with opening up to the realms of nature begins!

Remember the importance of your intention. This is you setting off on an adventure of receiving coaching from the realms of nature and the animal archetypes that work behind the scenes and hold the ropes for this realm. As with all visionary and shamanic enterprises, the only way is your own way. The warm-up of the last six chapters will have set you up with some structure and availability to connect in whatever way is true for you.

Now get ready, for the nature realms are ready to welcome you through their gates!

The following parts are set up to educate a pathway through four main nature communities. You can choose to work with them individually or read them all at the same time and then be open to the spectrum of whatever communicates with you. My recommendation would be to hold a focus with the nature community for each particular week, while knowing that everything is communicating all of the time so there may well be a particular other community that is waiting to break through and communicate with you too. Keep open but maintain focus.

The Way of Conversation

Even though I have given this section this name, I have to confess to not actually knowing what the way of conversation is. Or should I say if I know, then it is through a knowing that goes beyond my everyday knowing. As with all visionary practice, the way in is to be available to be educated by the "way". The process of becoming more and more available to following our own calling and honour the calling in everything else in these times includes undoing and releasing the plugs that condition our expectations about what conversation might look or feel like. The way of conversation for me has been found simply through surrendering to become available. I am constantly finding the portals to communication networks when I somehow let go, or through rituals I have set up that immerse me more and more in a different form to that which I apparently partake in while being a part of this tea party of human life.

Recently I have stopped being so passive about comments that I hear coming from a place of ignorance and prejudice. I recognize that my previous tolerance of comments putting down or brushing aside a nature-loving equal paradigm can be as damaging to the web of life as the saying of them in the first place. So I have just been practising the art of saying, "No, that's not true. It is possible to find ways of understanding that there is life and consciousness in everything." I have also started to spend more and more time in nature and with the weather or the night skies, listening. I have been thinking a lot about what it is that makes me happy. I know that when my passion to do this work begins to wane then I am not living my truth. It feels like what calls in me is that I need to be able to grow into who I truly am as a human in this lifetime. At the moment of writing, this looks like being a compassionate revolutionary against the constructs and the ideologies that restrict this. Being real and enjoying communion with what I have never before had chance to wholeheartedly commit to is what makes me happy. I know that nature is my teacher in this.

Restoring a natural way of being requires that we spend time allowing ourselves to be in a natural environment or in a more natural state of being. This can mean that we allow ourselves to be out in nature more, to be more aware of the elements in everything as we live our days, or that we keep coming back to feeling presence as our main practice. All of these entry points can lead us into a paradigm where interconnectedness and multi-sensory and multidimensional conversation just *is*.

Let us go with the idea that the way of conversation is found by being present, acknowledging the life in everything and then allowing.

EXERCISE
The Way of Conversation

This exercise will help you to attune to the way of conversation:
Take some minutes to sit and become at one with the weight of your body, the connection of your body with the Earth and the air about you and your relationship with the environment that you sit in right now.

Feel your breath as it rises from your lungs to your nostrils or mouth and back again. Feel yourself begin to relax as you welcome your relationship with your breathing and the meeting of the air of this world with your body, your spirit and your functioning as a human.

Become aware of the life in your environment that also depends on this air. Feel a place for stones, the Earth and all that grows in the Earth. Feel a place for water, running and still, and all that lives in the water and drinks or is washed by the water. Feel a place for fire, for the fire of our sun, for fires that burn within the Earth and on the Earth and for all that feel the fire within. Feel a place for air and the winds, for all the creatures that breathe the air and for all the creatures and man-made forms that can fly in the air. Feel a place for all of the planets, asteroids and stars that exist in space. Feel a place for you now, just as you are.

Acknowledge the life and the consciousness in everything and just be in this place for a few more minutes.

In this space of acknowledging and allowing, be present now to how you are feeling and sensing. Be in this space for just a few more minutes. Be open to whatever happens or arises in your mind, body, feelings or inner sight.

Come back and take some breaths. Make some notes or drawings on your experience.

Nature's Wisdom

I often think back to when I was at school in the 1970s. I was so happy then. I was happy because I was free to play most of the time. I played, I read, I felt a part of the seasons and the lovely rituals that life brought for its different times of the year. My life really was like a wheel of dependability and adventure. I can still remember the conversations I had with the many parts of nature that I grew up with. The wind in the grass was my favourite. Something so positive would open up to me when I was in this space with the grass and the wind playing together. I loved the different expressions that would come with different weathers and the feeling of there being a variety of spirits and beings occupying each of the many spaces on the land I visited. It was so obvious to me—I never questioned it—that the spirit of everything was communicating all of the time. I used to love writing stories and seeing what ideas would show up to weave with. I have no idea what the adults in my life were dealing with at that time. I just know that the space to be a child and have the connection with what was true and expressive was made freely available for me.

Nature is who we are. The Earth is who we are. When we are available to play with all aspects of creation, the creative spirit inside each of us becomes more alive and confident. We expand to be more than we think we are. We find our way. In the first weeks we worked with the idea that there are many different dimensions of expression. Every part of nature finds its way easily with all of the different dimensions of expression because each part of nature knows what it is. As mentioned in the nature section earlier, as humans we have our special way of being able to absorb and shape-shift and hold huge empathy for others. This can mean that we can become programmed, conditioned or overwhelmed or lose our sense of our innate way. Spending time in nature can really give us the opportunity to find our place in nature's wisdom to claim our unique essential way again.

EXERCISE

Plotting the Quest Spaces

For the visionary quest with nature, make a pact now with yourself that you will visit a place in nature at least three times over the next week or so, for half an hour or more.

Mark three spaces in your diary to clear the time for these visits.

You will have your special place with your tree as a base for you and as the headquarters for your visionary quest, but set yourself the task in this moment of making a list of places that have been calling you on the land for a while. You might have twelve places on your list or you might have just one or two that you return to. You might end up achieving visiting in person all twelve or find you visit just three repeatedly. Or you might find your two places take you in the end to visit others. It doesn't matter where you go. It just helps to make the appointment slots available and to begin to connect with important places consciously. This way the song lines can begin to open!

EXERCISE

Setting Up Your Tree Headquarters

Visit the tree that you located at the beginning of this book, where you read your intention and left something with it to represent your intention. Remind yourself of the intention you hold for Act 1: Calling.

Ask the tree if you can sit with it for a while.

Open up your senses as you did in the Way of Conversation exercise. When you get to the part of opening to acknowledging the life and consciousness in everything, focus especially on the tree. As you then reach the last minute of the allowing phase, ask that the tree opens up to you as a being and a spirit.

Just stay there open with your tree. Ask the tree to be an anchor and a balancer for you and see what happens. Know that you can go and sit with your tree at any point during the next months for balancing and for whatever you need. The tree will be a great helper for you on your visionary quest.

Setting Up the Boundaries for Your Visionary Quest and What to Expect

A Vision Quest is a bit like entering into a story. It holds a beginning, middle and ending. A Vision Quest will follow the traditional structure of: beginning—separation from the known; middle—a period of isolation; and ending—the return. So the key here, over a longer period of time Vision Questing, is that there will be sacred moments in your life where you are open to the insertion of this narrative of separation from the known, open to a period of isolation and open to returning. This is the purpose of your setting points in your diary to ensure you will be available for these quests. Obviously, the shorter timescale allows for a less deep immersion, but one of the purposes of this book is to insert the truth that our lives are visioning for us all of the time, that everything is open to communicate with us and that we are living in a world theatre that is full of opportunities for divination and healing.

In the traditional Vision Quest, one would enter a solitary space of prayer, meditation, stillness and focus. This would then open up to the guidance of the wider self of the cosmos coming to greet us.

A Vision Quest is a rite of passage that helps awaken us to the profound unity of all life. As a part of many traditions all around the world for thousands of years, it is one of the most powerful ways to contact guidance, inspiration and renewal.

When you set out on each mini quest or pilgrimage, set yourself a small opening ceremony to show your availability to guidance and changing of form in line with the intention that you hold. Set the intention that you will easily return to the everyday and find your place in your everyday life again.

Be aware that messages and insights will be more likely to come through outside of the allotted time too. So you will feel yourself a part of a continuum. But also, be aware that you are not here to continuously quest or look for meaning in everything. That is not what this work is about. The visionary path is one of being able to live the vibration of which you truly are and to feel present, connected and in your life on this planet. It is to just partake and be in life. Try not to strive or feel like you are on some important mission. Do what keeps you happy and grounded outside of the quest time. When you are on your official quest time, try to see it that these openings are set up to feed and bring even more joy in life to your everyday experience of living.

A Visionary Quest can bring up a lot. It is important to know how to sign in and out and how to put boundaries up for yourself so that you can go back into your everyday life. As much as setting time in your diary to be available to quest with your visionary nature, also set time to just have space to do things like clean your house, your car, meet friends for coffee and go to the cinema. Self-care is key.

Some of the things that a visionary quest of this nature may bring up are: emotions that need to be felt, information that is buried in the tribal or world soul that needs to be acknowledged, visions to be woven into the future, healing moments, spirits that your own soul has been waiting for a long time to meet, insights, impressions, dark sorrow and a whole range of difficult material that may have been buried by the trauma or misplaced shame of your ancestors.

It might be that these things come up for you while you are out in nature. However, it may also be that instead your dreams reveal a lot or you become more emotional in your everyday life, for example. A good plan is to give yourself an hour a week to journal or speak with a friend about what is coming up for you. But give yourself set times for this so that you are not swimming in the process but letting the river flow to appointed times when you can release and bring special attention to yourself.

Visionary Quest Opening Ceremony

In this opening ceremony, what you are doing is in effect just honouring and inviting all that is supportive or important information in the seen and unseen realms to be with you. You are opening up the "wholeness template". As you know, this is called the medicine wheel in many traditions. It is a circle of inclusivity and includes the four directions and the four elements that constitute both the map of our bearings and the elements that make us manifest in the physical realms. It holds medicine because it bears information as well as the quality of deep listening that permits a healing remedy to be found. The template also works multidimensionally when we bring in the central axis that is the present moment as it meets the horizontal wheel. Above and below this are all different times and spaces that hold the vibration of the frequencies of being. You can also see the central axis as moving around to be a full circle and to hold an eternal flow of the multidimensional worlds. Feel this click into place as an over- and under-arch that creates an orb with the horizontal ring. And then there you are, walking around with the whole of everything as an orb blessing your path.

1 If it feels right to, you can shake a rattle and whistle to call in the four directions and the elements. You can also be silent in doing this if that feels more comfortable for you. Feel a circle all around you moving through anchors for each of the four directions. Now whistle or rattle or bring your attention quietly to the centre and the upper and the lower parts of this axis. Feel the different frequencies included in this line. Allow the line to bend and to become an eternal flow as it then moves out as a disc to meet the horizontal axis circle and become an orb.

2 Connect with your heart and stand in stillness. Appreciate the stillness where you stand in the centre of this great circle and sphere. Feel the inner knowing that you are guided on your quest and that your quest to know yourself more truly and serve your intention benefits the way of being for all. Feel gratitude.

3 Call in your guide from nature, your pathfinder guide and your Protector. Feel them with you. Your space is now ready.

At the end of each visionary quest session, thank everything that has held you. Take notes and then release yourself and everything from the session, while knowing that everything is actually always holding you all of the time.

Chapter 7

Weather Spirits

Focus: The Practice of Working with the Weather Spirits

The forces of nature have a dramatic effect on our lives. Whether the sun is shining brightly in the sky or a stormy wind blows, the atmosphere that the weather provides can both colour our moods and bring movement to our states of being. Weather brings insight, messages, the power to heal and often revelations.

When we begin to open up more to our availability to get to know the weather and its different agents, then we start a relationship with them that allows communication channels to open.

You can imagine that weather communication would have been a natural practice inherent to all cultures in the times when humans and the spirit of all things communicated together. Alexander Carmichael, who spent fifty years collecting legends, songs, curses and oral history from Gaelic-speakers, recorded these words about the practices of Scottish Highlanders in the 1800s: "The old people had runes which they sang to the spirits dwelling in the sea and in the mountains, in the wind and in the whirl-wind, in the lightning and in the thunder, in the sun and in the moon and in the stars of heaven."[5]

The Koyukon people of Alaska, in noticing the crows coming to be fed by people, attribute this apparent imbalance to the loss of those able to work with the spirits of the animals and the elemental forces of nature.[6]

---

5 A. Carmichael, A. Matheson, J. Carmichael Watson & E. C. Carmichael Watson, *Carmina Gadelica* (Edinburgh: Scottish Academic Press, 1928).
6 Moss, N. and Corbin, D., *Weather Shamanism* (Vermont: Inner Traditions, 2008).

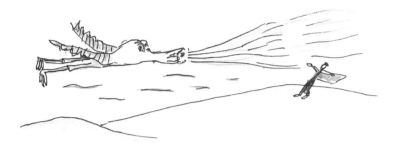

The feature of rainfall after important ceremonies or prayers is well known through many traditions. Plutarch, one of the philosophers of Ancient Greece, noted in his writings that heavy rains often fell on major battle sites once the fighting was over.

The Hopi of south-western America are acknowledged for their success in rainmaking.

Working and communicating in a heart-opening and authentic way with the spirits of the weather offers the key to bringing balance and redistribution of power through the web of our world.

Below are names of some of the spirits of the weather. First there is a list of weather gods and goddesses of Ancient Greece. This is followed by a generic list of weather spirits from many traditions.

I recommend that when you work with the weather spirits you refer to these lists for inspiration. Please feel free to change their gender, make them androgynous or change their names. It is always best in your own practice to ask the weather spirits as you meet them what they would like you to call each of them and work with the first answers you are given.

Ancient Greek Weather Gods and Goddesses

The list below shows how the seasons, weather and stars are an orchestra together and gives you some idea of how the Ancient Greeks would have digested and placed the meaning of weather. I hope reading about them here helps you to get a sense of this in yourself.

Aeolus is the king of the winds. He was appointed by Zeus to guard the storm winds.

Aether is the primeval god of the shining light of the blue sky. He was conceived of as the substance of light that is a layer of bright mist lying between the dome of heaven and the lower air surrounding the earth.

The Amemi are the gods of the four directional winds and the heralds of the four seasons.

The Anemoi are the Daemones of the violent storm winds.

Arce is the messenger of the Titans. She is the sister of Iris and the goddess of the lost second rainbow.

The Astra Planeta are gods of the five wandering stars or planets. The leader of these is Eosphoros, who is the god of the dawn star Venus. The other four are Pyroeis (Mars), Phaenon (Saturn), Phaethon (Jupiter) and Stilbon (Mercury).

Astraeus is the Titan god of the stars. He is father of the planets and the four seasonal winds by Eos the dawn.

Astrape is lightning.

Astrothesiai are spirits or living forms of the heavenly constellations. They are mainly heroes and creatures placed among the stars by the gods as a reward for some service or as a memorial of their crimes.

Atlas is a Titan who was famously condemned by Zeus to hold the sky aloft upon his shoulders and turn it upon its axis. He was released from this labour and appointed keeper of the pillars of heaven.

Aura is the Titan goddess of the breeze.

Aurae are the nymphs of the breezes.

Boreas is the god of the north wind, whose wintry breath brings the cold of winter. He dwells in a cave in the mountains of the far northern land of Thrace.

Chaos is the primeval goddess of the gap between heaven and earth. She is the air we breathe. Chaos is the mother of Darkness and Night and of the birds.

Chione is the goddess of snow. She is the daughter of Boreas, god of the wintry north wind.

Chronos is the old god of time who turned the wheel of the heavenly constellations. Sometimes he is equated with Cronus, the father of Zeus.

The Cyclopes (Kyklopes) are three giant sons of Uranus (Heaven) who forge the lightning and thunder of Zeus.

Eophorus (Eosphoros) is the god of the dawn star (the star Venus) seen in the morning skies. He was originally regarded as being distinct from Hesperus, the god of the evening star.

Eos is the winged goddess of the dawn. She heralds the rising of the sun with her rosy brilliance.

Eurus (Euros) is the god of the east wind and herald of the autumn season.

Harpyaie (Harpyiai) are daemones of whirlwinds and storm gusts. They are known as the hounds of Zeus and are thought to be responsible for the disappearance of people without a trace.

Hecatoncheires (Hekatonkheires) are three hundred-armed, fifty-headed giants. They are the gods of violent storms.

Helius (Helios) is the god of the sun, whose orb he wears upon his head as a bright aureole crown. Helios drives a fiery chariot drawn by four winged horses.

Hemera is the primeval goddess of the day. In the early morn she scatters the mists of her mother Nyx (Lady Night), to reveal the shining light of Aether, the blue sky.

Hera is the Queen of Heaven and goddess of the air and starry constellations. The Milky Way was spilled from her breast.

Herse is the goddess of the morning dew.

Hesperides are the goddesses of sunsets. The three Hesperides tend the tree of the golden apples on Erythea, the Red Isle, in the western stream of the river Oceanus. They are the source of the golden light of sunset, created to celebrate the nuptials of the sky gods.

Hesperus (Hesperos) is the god of the evening star (the planet Venus). He was originally distinct from his stellar counterpart Eophorus, the dawn star.

Horae (1) (Horai) are three goddesses of the seasons and the ordering of time named Eirene, Eunomia and Dike. They direct the constellations and guide the sun in his heavenly course.

Horae (2) (Horai) are the goddesses of the twelve hours of the day. They were originally the same as the first three mentioned above.

Hyades are nymphs of the five stars of the constellation Hyades. They are daughters of the Titan Atlas.

Iris is the goddess of the rainbow and the messenger of the Olympian gods.

Menae are the nymphs of the fifty new moons of the Olympiad (a period of four years). Fifty moons are significant because this number marked the conjunction of solar and lunar calendars.

Nephelae (Nephelai) are the nymphs of the clouds. They are daughters of the earth-encircling river Oceanus, from whose waters they draw rain.

Notus (Notos) is the god of the wet and stormy south wind who heralds the month of summer.

Nyx is the primeval goddess of night. In the evening Nyx draws her curtain of dark mists across the sky, cloaking the light of her son Aether, the shining blue sky. In the morn, her daughter Hemera (the goddess Day) lifts the dark mantle.

Oceanides (Okeanides) are the daughters of the Earth-encircling river Oceanus. Some of these are nymphs of clouds (Nephelae) and moistening breezes (Aurae).

Oreithyia is the goddess of cold, gusty mountain winds. She is the wife of Boreas, the wintry north wind, and the mother of Chione, snow.

Pleiades are the nymphs of the seven stars of the constellation Pleiades. They are daughters of the Titan Atlas and their rising and setting were of key importance in the agricultural calendar.

Selene is the goddess of the moon. She rides across the sky on the back of a bull or an ass, or in a chariot drawn by winged horses.

Uranus (Ouranos) is the primeval god whose body forms the solid dome of heaven.

Zephirus (Zephyros) is the god of the gentle west wind and the herald of spring. He is the husband of Chloris, the goddess of flowers, and the father of Carpus, fruits.

Zeus is the King of the Gods and the ruler of the heavens. He is the god of clouds, rain, thunder and lightning.

Zodiac (Zodiakos) are the spirits of the twelve constellations of the zodiac that circle heaven, measuring the seasons of the year.

The Great Winds

Amihan: Tagalog and Visayan (Philippine) god of the cool, northeast wind.

Biegkegaellies: Sami god of winter winds and storms.

Cihuatecayoti: Aztec god of the west wind.

Circios: Greek god of the north-northeast wind.

Dogoda: Slavic god of quiet pleasant wind and clear weather.

Egoi: Basque god of the south wind.

Ehecatl: Aztec god of wind.

Enlil: Sumerian god of air and storms.

Erebos: Greek god of the southeast wind.

Euronotus: Greek god of the southwest wind.

Favonius: Roman god of the west wind.

Fei Lian: Chinese (Taoist) god of wind. Human form is Feng Bo.

Fujin: Japanese god of the wind. One of the oldest Shinto gods.

Gaoh: Iroquois spirit master of the winds.

Guabancex: Native American (Taino) storm goddess.

Kahit: Native American (Kahit) wind god.

Kaikias: The Greek god of the northeast wind.

Kon: Incan god of rain and wind.

Lips: The Greek god of the southwest wind.

Menuo: Lithuanian god of the east wind.

Mictianpachecati: Aztec god of the north wind.

Negafook: Inuit god of weather systems—represents the north wind.

Niltsi: Native American (Navajo) wind god.

Ninlil: Sumerian (Mesopotamian) goddess of the wind—consort of Enlil.

Njoror: Norse god of the wind and sea.

Novensiles: Nine Roman gods of lightning.

Nuada: Celtic god of sky, wind and war.

Oonawith Unggi: Native American (Cherokee) ancient spirit of the wind.

Oya: Yoruban deity of winds, lightning and violent storms.

O-yan-do-ne: The moose spirit of the east wind.

Pauahtuns: Mayan wind gods.

Perun: Slavic god of thunder, lightning and wind.

Pietys: Lithuanian god of the south wind.

Qebui: Egyptian god of the north wind. Appears as a ram with four heads.

Quetzalcoatl: Aztec god of wind.

Q'ug'umatz: Mayan god of wind and rain.

Rudra: Vedic wind or storm god.

Rytys: Lithuanian god of the east wind.

Shinatsuhiko: Japanese goddess of wind.

Shu: Egyptian god of the wind and air.

Siaurys: Lithuanian god of the north wind.

Silla: Native American (Inuit) god of the sky, wind and the weather. Also called **Silap Inua**.

Stribog: Slavic god and spirit of the winds, sky and air.

Szelatya: Hungarian god of wind.

Takaris: Lithuanian god of the west wind.

Tate: Native American (Lakota) wind god or spirit.

Tawhiri: Maori (ancient New Zealand) god of weather including thunder, lightning, wind, clouds and storms.

Tezcatlipoca: Aztec god of hurricanes and night wind.

Tialocayoti: Aztec god of the east wind.

Varpulis: Slavic god of storm winds.

Varuna: Hindu god of the sky.

Vayu-Vata: Avestan (Persian) wind god.

Venti: Roman wind gods who were each ascribed a cardinal direction from which the winds blew.

Vitzlampaehecati: Aztec god of the south wind.

Wayra Tata: Puruha Quechuas (and Aymaras) god associated with hurricane winds.

Waziya: Native American (Lakota) giant of the north winds who guards the aurora borealis and controls ice and snow.

Wiyohipeyata: Native American (Lakota) god or spirit of the west winds.

Wiyohiyanpa: Native American (Lakota) god or spirit of the east winds.

Ya-o-gah: Native American (Iroquois) destructive bear spirit of the north wind.

Yaponcha: Native American (Hopi) wind god.

Setting Up the Earth Whisperer Practice

Your task is simply to open space for your visionary quest time in the usual way suggested earlier, and then to visit your chosen place for your quest, holding particular attention to the weather.

EXERCISE

Weather Calling

Be in nature with the weather happening around you. Which members of the world of weather are you noticing at work right now? Perhaps it is the wind and the sun shining. Maybe you feel a still air holding the space but spot the approach of a storm by the storm clouds in the distance.

In your body, feel into a part of yourself that is a receiver for the weather spirits. You will notice that this part of you feels a stirring or gentle opening when you tune in to the weather. I feel this part that is receiving in my chest. It is almost as if I have a receiver in my heart centre, in the same place as the speaker in one of those dolls I used to have as a child that I would pull the string from to make her talk.

The receiver opens and I feel my eyes begin to move about in their sockets as I concentrate on making a space for the weather in my environment to communicate with me. I search out and see what part of the weather team is most available to me right now in this moment. As I write, the sun calls. I listen with my heart to the sun and ask the calling of the sun to meet the calling in me. Then I am just remaining open and allowing what needs to flow to flow.

EXERCISE

Weather Responding

In these sacred moments with the weather spirit getting to know how it communicates and is, you can make a connection with the spirit by asking yourself what colour, temperature, volume and size the weather spirit has. If you were to find a colour to relate to how you feel it, what would it be? If you were to find a volume how quiet or loud is it? What is the weather spirit's tone? Is it soft or sharp? Dull or distinct? If it was a musical instrument what instrument would it be? In this way build up an idea of the form of the spirit. Also, be open to breaking this down at any point if it starts to prevent you from having a clear connection with the soul of the spirit of the weather. You can ask for a name when you feel ready.

See if you can make some colour drawings of the weather spirit. See if you can record what you are feeling the weather spirit communicating.

Remember the objective is for the calling in you to meet the calling in the weather spirit and have a meeting together.

How does the weather spirit respond to your calling?

What do you feel as the calling of the weather spirit? Find a way to show the weather spirit that you hear its Calling. You don't need to do anything except hear it and let it be a part of everything. Being open will create a movement.

You can also go out into the weather and ask the weather to bring you just what you need. See what happens.

Ask the weather to communicate to you what it most needs to express. See what happens.

See if any random movements appear during the week to do with the weather.

Make notes on your experiences with the weather.

At the end of your time with the weather, thank the weather spirit or spirits you have communicated with and thank those you haven't yet opened to. Know that you have opened up a practice that has the potential to develop further.

Chapter 8

Birds

Focus: Birds and Their Meanings

The birds have always been great messengers for the people. There are various augury practices, recorded through time, of people working with the birds, from the Chinese tradition of crow divination to the Ancient Roman practice of reading flight patterns.

Birds have been known to take on the role of teachers, guardians, role models, counsellors, healers, jesters, bringers of peace and meteorologists. They are honoured as carriers of messages and warnings from loved ones and the spirit world; they often report or bring omens of deaths and injuries. They seem to channel divine intelligence to answer our important questions. Their signs can be both subtle and dramatic.

Bird imagery as a shamanic messenger is prevalent in modern, ancient and primal art. The egg is a symbol prevalent in many ancient cultures and is shown as an oval or a circle. It is found drawn on stones, petroglyph rock art, pottery and ancient buildings, conveying imagery of the birthing of life. The Goddess as bird, for example as the crane or owl in Scottish tradition as familiars of the Cailleach, and as the vulture in Egyptian and Mediterranean traditions, marks the meaning of the goddess as a female

elder archetype that traverses the gap between life and death and brings forth eternal life. The frame drum can be as much felt as the dying and reborn moon as the egg membrane from which life will return and through which that which is beyond life can speak and be known.

The significance of the birds' ability to fly high and reach heights not physically possible for humans gives birds a perspective in our world and makes birds symbolic of the ability to move beyond the field of ordinary existence through the air element. Their relationship with the weather and the trees is particularly strong. Bird symbols are used as logos by various organizations. You know some of these! Like Twitter, Penguin Books and Dove beauty products.

Setting Up the Earth Whisperer Practice

A good way to understand the significance of different birds and their relationship to you and your calling is to be present when they appear and then begin to attune to them and allow yourself to imagine yourself as being them.

EXERCISE

Bird Calling

Set yourself up ready to go on your visionary quest session. Connect with the calling you hold for this Act, or the genuine feeling or longing that you are connected with right now. Become present and aware of the air and the Earth in particular. Let yourself open to the world of birds. Put down some offerings for the birds (seeds or specially bought bird food). Honour the birds everywhere. Feel your Protector, your nature guide and your pathfinder with you. Let yourself just stay in tune with what you hold authentically in this moment and whatever wants to surface in the world around you. Hold no attachment to an idea.

You can also hold an area that is longing for healing in your life at the moment or a particular grief that you feel for someone or something, and be open to the birds bringing healing or an important meeting.

EXERCISE
Bird Responding

If a bird appears, then pause and be open to making a connection with it. Feel in your body where you connect with the bird's being. Wear your Protector. Allow yourself to open up so that you can accommodate the feeling of being this particular bird right now. Feel its character and its way. Be open to feel the quality that the bird holds and the way in which it senses the world.

Ask the bird what it wants you to know right now and see what comes.

If the bird fleetingly flies past but doesn't linger, then be open to it as a sign. See what you were thinking or feeling at the sign of its appearance. Tune in to the bird and ask in yourself what you already know inside as the quality the bird brings for you.

If you are putting out for healing or for the meeting of grief, be curious about which bird arrives in response to this and ask yourself internally to be open to the healing and the connection. Try not to use your mind but allow your availability to receive medicine and meaning in a deeper way to feel the truth of the rendezvous that occurs in response to your request.

Ask the bird what it knows and what it needs you to know from it right now.

Write notes after each outing.

If nothing comes, don't worry—the appointment was made. Be open to your dreams or another time bringing the bird and its message through.

At the end of the time with birds, feed the birds and thank them for their being there. Continue to feed the birds over the following weeks.

Chapter 9

Trees

Focus: Trees and Their Lore

Now we enter into the wonderful world of trees! In the Ogham, the medieval system of the Irish and Pictish Druids, the major trees and their sounds became the alphabet sounds. It is nice to think that we speak and communicate with the sounds of the trees.

Lore is a word that is used to describe the ancient information and knowledge that has been passed down (mainly orally) through different traditions. Tree lore speaks about the qualities, medicine and ways of listening of the many different trees. Our ancestors will have known well that each tree holds a particular role for us. Sitting with trees and attuning to them can bring much wisdom and healing through.

Trees play an important part in many myths. In many stories of trees, they are known to be the home of spirits. Trees have many meanings and some are universally known, while others may be specific to a certain group. The ancient symbol of the tree has been found to represent physical and spiritual nourishment and transformation. Carl Jung wrote about how the tree symbolized self, androgyny, and equality between the sexes and individuation.

∧ ∨ ∧

Here is a list of trees that may act as a jumping-off point for your own connections and insights. Remember that the information you divine from your own connection far supersedes what any written information can bring.

Apple: magic, youth, simple order
Ash: sacrifice, higher awareness and power
Aspen: determination, blessings, overcoming fears and doubts
Beech: tolerance, past knowledge, elf connections

Birch: new beginnings, cleansing of past, Vision Quests
Cedar: healing, cleansing, protection
Cherry: death and rebirth, new awakenings
Cypress: understanding the role of sacrifice
Elder: birth and death, fairy realm
Elm: strength of will, intuition
Hazel: hidden wisdom, dousing, divination
Holly: protection, overcoming of anger, spiritual openings
Oak: holding the order, strength, light within
Palm: peace and opportunity
Pine: creativity, life, longevity, immortality
Willow: feminine transmission, healing, inner vision, dreams
Yew: ancient wisdom, connection with the ancestors, death

Setting Up the Earth Whisperer Practice

The practice this week will be to be open to which of the trees call you. You may have already begun to notice certain trees that feel like they are appearing for you. Hold your intention for Act 1: Calling and go out on a walk. Be discerning and see which tree is answering the calling of the quest you personally hold within.

Also, start to be aware of when certain kinds of trees appear to you in your everyday life and be in the habit of greeting them and getting to know what family of trees they belong with.

✺

EXERCISE

Tree Meeting

When you have discerned the tree that is answering the call of the quest you hold within, approach it and ask it if you can sit or stand with it for a while. Touch the trunk, branches, leaves if they are there, and feel the energy of the tree through your hands and your body. Feel how its roots sink deep into the ground and how its branches stretch out. Notice whether you have been drawn to a small or young tree or a tall or old one. What is the significance of the size or age of the tree for you?

Now just let the tree see you. Imagine yourself as if you are naked and have nothing to hide. How does it feel to allow yourself to be seen by a member of nature? See how easily you are able to expose your soul. As you open to the tree, be aware of how much is real about what you carry and how much is illusion or falsity.

Allow the tree to bring you into a more sure relationship with your truth.

EXERCISE

Tree Understanding

In turn, open up now to the tree being able to show itself to you. As you are connected with the pulse of its life force and being, be open to receiving it as a spirit by being available to hear its deep knowing. See what comes. Bear witness.

If there is anything that feels like it is needed for you and for the tree, then ask to be connected to the universal energy through the tree and be open to the accessing of this by whatever is feeling like it is needing support or deeper listening.

Step back and give thanks to the tree you have connected with. Make some notes. What are you feeling like now?

At the end of your time with trees, sign out with them and honour them by singing them a song. Know that you remain open to connection at the right time for you and the trees now.

Chapter 10

Focus: The Fae (or Sidhe) and Scottish Tradition

I like to think of the fae, or the world of fairy, as being the transmission realm between nature and humans. The fae hold a territory that is full of energy and stories, much as is the human realm. The human and the fae realms interact.

Once you start to include the fae intentionally a lot can open up. I have held the most beautiful Beltane fire walk evenings where we open up to join the fae groups as humans. Perceptions of reality can shift dramatically in this week. Prepare yourself for an opening! Also, strange things can happen that don't seem to make sense. I had a year working with the fae on a story project and all sorts of information and changes would appear on my phone screen. Texts would send that I hadn't written and words that I spoke would be received in a different way. I learnt a lot about interfaces and story fields within the nature, human and fairy stations. Now I understand my place a lot better within each of these realms and have cleared some programmes, things are much smoother. I also take things slowly and set clear intentions that I need to keep my clear belonging in the human while opening to communication with the fae.

Have a think about your boundaries before you step into the exercises for this week. I am setting the overarching intention for everyone that we each work at a steady rate and with the intention of gentle healing and understanding.

Opening to the fae can bring an extra dimension of life, liveliness and connectivity. It can also speed up manifestation projects. It can bring to the surface some plots for healing. You can find all sorts in the fairy realm, including tampering energy. So the best thing to do to begin is to honour this realm and state that you are looking to connect simply to be present for one another and not to serve one another in any way.

The term "fae", incidentally, can include the elementals, although the elementals also have a place of their own. The different plant species each hold fae as a spiritual dimension. The tree spirits can hold a place with the fae as dryads.

The fae work and position themselves within the elements just like we do. Below are the schools of fairy that work with air, fire, water and earth. Following on from this you can read about the different members of the fairy worlds. Feel free to make your own mind up and change the meanings if they don't resonate with you. As these are just translations of information accessed through time, asking the fae direct will give you the best information.

Air Spirits: Silfides.
Water Spirits: Nymphs, Mermaids, Nereids, Naiads, Undines and Water Goblins.
Earth Spirits: Ladies, Goblins, Gnomes and Trolls.
Fire Spirits: Salamanders, Farralis, Ra-arus and Dragons.

Fae, like the weather spirits we looked at earlier, are known all over the world in many different cultures.

Abatwa: From South African culture; they are very small.
Ballybogs: Ireland. Similar faeries known as bogles are also found in Welsh and Cornish faery lore. They live around peat bogs or mud holes and are small mud-covered creatures.

The Banshee: Ireland. An ancestral spirit appointed to forewarn members of certain ancient families of their time of death. They can appear in one of three guises: a young woman, a stately matron or a raddled old hag.

Brown Men: Scotland. An elemental of fire.

Brownies: England. Earth elementals.

Clurichaun: Ireland. Similar fairies are found in Italy by the name of Monciello.

Dryads: Greece. Their element is air. They appear as wispy lights that are seen in old trees.

Ellyllon: Wales. Water is their element; jovial and happy.

Elves: Northern Europe. Light Elves are translucent and blue-coloured. Dark Elves build their homes beneath the earth.

Erluitle: Switzerland. Associated with the Earth.

Gnomes: Europe. Earth spirits.

Goblins: Europe including Scandinavia, UK and France.

Imps: Germany. They have a lot of playful energy.

Kelpies: Scotland. Water elementals that are a cross between a horse, a waterfowl and a wildcat.

Leprechauns: Ireland. From the Irish *leath bhrogan* (shoemaker).

Menehunas: Hawaii. Earth spirits.

The Merrows (a type of Selkie): Ireland. *Muir* (meaning sea) and *oigh* (meaning maid).

Nymphs: Greece. Nymphs are associated with the element of whatever they inhabit. They appear as women of nature.

Pixies: Scotland. Characterized by having very large eyes, wings, pointy ears and noses and big eyebrows.

Red Caps: Scotland. Associated with fire.

Tengu: Japan. Air spirits.

The Tuatha de Danann: Ireland. Trooping fairies.

Undines: Middle East. Water spirits—human and seahorse with a human head.

Well Spirits: Ireland, England and Norway. They are shape-shifters who can take the form of human beings.

Will 'o' Wisp: Ireland. Fairy lights, known to be quiet and helpful. They appear in the misty Irish mountains to help searchers locate someone lost.

Zips: Mexico. Earth spirits. Their sole function is to assist forest creatures, mainly deer.

Setting Up the Earth Whisperer Practice

Your practice will be to hold the calling you hold within as your intention for this book and then be open to allowing the fae to show their selves to you and to get to know them.

☙

EXERCISE

Fae Meeting

First of all set the intention that you only do the below for twenty minutes and then come back to the everyday.

Wearing your Protector and travelling with your guide from nature and your pathfinder guide, go and sit in nature somewhere. Hold your intention for the course in your heart and then allow yourself to attune to operating at your fae frequency. Ask the fae to meet you at this frequency. Notice how your body feels and how your eyesight and hearing changes as you do this. Notice openings and shifts in perception.

After twenty minutes come back to the present and spend ten minutes grounding, stamping, running and being with the Earth to return fully to this realm again.

☙

EXERCISE

Fae Opening to Vision

Ask the fae to let you have a vision of their Calling and their perfect way of being with humans in this world.

See what visions open to you.

Make drawings and recordings of this. Let the fae know that you cherish this information.

Leave offerings for the fae.

At the end of your time with the fae, close down the intensive connection but know that the fae will continue to appear to you from time to time at times that are convenient and right for both of you.

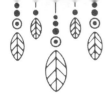

Scene 4: Animals and Archetypal Support Systems

Review

It has possibly been quite a journey so far! You have traversed the territories of Prep, Tuning and Nature's Communications. As much as being an opening to what is true, you will have noticed that following Calling is also a process of releasing deeply embedded conditioning and the unconscious acceptances of relationships and environments. This can feel a very energetic process! As our truer and more innate nature comes through within ourselves and the wider worlds it can feel like a great love affair. But like a great love affair, it may unintentionally sweep us off of our feet! As disowned parts of ourselves come back into the play of life again, we are able to feel, love and care more deeply about what is true. So, it is a good idea at this stage to take a step back and have a review.

I recommend that you spend a couple of days reflecting on where you have been and what has been happening for you before you embark on your journey into Animals and Archetypal Support Systems.

Visit the special tree that you set up a relationship with at the beginning of this book. Take your time to be with presence. Remember the Visionary triangle of knowing, nature and trust. Open up to connect with your own true knowing and the wider wisdom. Be with nature and feel into the wisdom of this Earth and all of its members. Lean back against your tree and attune to trust. How is trust in you now that you have spent these last two months on your visionary quest with tuning and nature?

What is changing in you? What is becoming more certain and established? What is changing in your relationship with your sense of self as a part of nature? That's right: your relationship with your sense of self as a part of nature. What is that part of you that relates with your sense of self? Your whole relationship with how you have been conditioned to think about yourself will be changing and adjusting. It is possible that there will be a shell of the old self that will begin to drop off and a new formation for mapping yourself will be forming. It might feel like an archaeological dig of a deeper and more authentic self. The part of you that wasn't previously allowed to take the driving seat is now starting to drive. Your sense of self will be able to ally more with the part of you that connects with nature and the other dimensions of existence. Your world is expanding.

In turn, think about your relationships with your family and community. What is changing in your relationships? What do you need more of to be able to be you? What do your family and friends need from you so that you can direct an even more authentic alliance with those you love and care for? It is likely that you will need to have a lot of patience and compassion for all of your relationships. It is likely that you will need to both protect your inner journey and also be skilful and gentle in the way you communicate.

As you sit with your tree, think about the quantum field idea that everything is affecting everything else all of the time. Think back to how being available to be multidimensional and a part of nature has supported you to make some changes. Be aware that your presence will be affecting your family and community also. How is that feeling? Where are you noticing that extra support is needed to help bring harmony and ease? Feel into your tree and the whole of nature and allow yourself to vision any of these relationships or environments with the supporting inclusion of the worlds you are coming to know better.

When you feel complete and more settled, thank your tree for its availability to hold space with you. Return to your life, knowing that you can call on this extra support at any time. You are not alone!

Animal and Archetypal Realms Here We Come!

The time to investigate the land of the animals and archetypes begins!

Behind this everyday manifestation of life is another realm that influences and interplays with it. This realm constitutes what is sometimes known as the mythical world. It is occupied by what we know as animal archetypes or deities. Different cultures have their own versions of what this mythical realm is.

In Celtic mythology, the Otherworld is the realm of the animal archetypes, the deities and also of the dead. In Greek mythology the underworld is the realm of Hades. It is the feminine Persephone who takes the cycle from the everyday worlds into there. In Egyptian cosmology, myth is the realm of Osiris and Isis opens the doors into this. In Roman mythology it is the realm of Pluto and it is Proserpine who makes the descent.

I love the Greek description, here below, of those who stand in front of the entrance to the underworld. I feel it really helps to see that the mythical beings who are the openers to this realm are actually also the emotions we feel in everyday life.

Those who hold stations at the gates are:

Grief (Penthos)	Fear (Phobos)	Agony (Algea)
Anxiety (Cure)	Hunger (Limos)	Sleep (Hypnos)
Diseases (Nosoi)	Need (Aporia)	Guilty Joys (Gaudia)
Old Age (Geras)	Death (Thanatos)	

On the opposite threshold is:

War (Polemos)	Fury (Erinyes)	Discord (Eris)

Close to the doors are many beasts, including:

Centaurs	Gorgons	Chimera
Scylla	Lernaean Hydra	Harpies
Briareus	Geryon	

In the midst of all these mythical beings in the story of the ones at the thresholds is an elm tree. The tree harbours false dreams (oneiroi) and they cling under every leaf.

Doesn't this help us to see that in every edge of separation, fear or strong emotional state is an entry point to the worlds beyond this one? Consider this in your journey with the animals and archetypal support systems and I think you will find you are opening or slamming shut the doors to these potential meetings with the other worlds at so many points through your life! The job in this chapter is to acknowledge the gift and the power of these edges and to allow the doors to open.

Archetypal Landscapes

Years ago, when I was journeying with fire in a ceremony to divine my "mission" with my work, a dragon came through the heat and the flames to meet me. Dragon conveyed how one of my roles was to work with theatre and the dragon lines of the earth. The message was that I was to set up a theatre visiting the different sites of the land to work with the mythical worlds and the archetypes. My guidance was that there were certain myths that needed healing and that the mythical worlds needed the world of humans to intervene to be able to heal the archetypes and myths.

This blew my mind. It was empowering and humbling for me to hear. I duly set up Dragon Theatre and spent ten years working on projects that culminated in a Year of Myth project in 2015. I found myself moving to a place called Wormit, which means the Place of the Dragon. My house was right on the side of Dragon Hill. I climbed the hill and journeyed deep into the mythology of the land there for the eight years I lived and dreamt there and brought through many art and theatre healing projects. Through the reliving of a certain story of the land of Scotland and by listening to the story within my own living landscape, I was able to access and open to the reality that we do indeed live the entrenched codes and permeations of the land and the stories of the land on which we live. I discovered for true that we do have the doors to be able to communicate and work in healing ways with the keyholders of these patterns through myth. Sometimes myth is handed to us through lore and passed down through oral tradition. Often we can tap into the myth by opening to create and draw, sing, speak or write the stories out.

What we encounter in ourselves when we open this flow is a deep creative pool that is the archive of healing, flowing light. What is more, this healing, flowing light moves in both directions. We find we are not puppets to the forces and the worlds behind us but rather supporters of a flow of a way of life that brings nourishment on all levels. The creator within can be awakened as well as the creator without. I truly believe that calling is in both camps and in the end they are both one. If we can bring both together again then we can enter both a new and an ancient paradigm that goes far beyond the fighting and warlike state that both our myths and our everyday lives have us believe we are trapped in. There is absolutely no trace of weapons used for fighting in the artefacts from Paleolithic times. Warlessness is thought by many to have been a possible state of being until the appearance of *Homo sapiens* some 315,000 years ago. Through my own journeys I see the guidance that supports the notion of there being a period of "Paleolithic warlessness".

The mythical realm can be seen as a disc that surrounds the planes of this existence. It contains animal archetypes. These animals each correlate with the god and goddess archetypes that are particular to different traditions. Jung described the archetypes as being the highest developed elements of what he called the collective unconscious. He saw how they served to interact and call upon a divine working of the universal web in a specific way. In the Visionary model, we tap into this and open to seeing how this interplay happens. A lot of indigenous and shamanic cultures consider animal archetypes to be guides to universal organizing principles and acknowledge the power they have to orchestrate the world around. You can begin to appreciate from this the power of animal archetypes as keyholders and their individual accessing of specific domains of power.

If you think about yourself and your own calling and the area of interest you hold central in this lifetime, you might be able to perceive how there are certain animal archetypes and archetypal expressions that are close to your soul. We will see through the next chapters just how much the animals and archetypes have roles in the wheel of life and creative flow. You will also come to find which ones are particularly important for you and the ones you are called to heal with.

The choosing of the animal archetypes defines how an entire culture chooses to empower and manifest their world. The mythical realm supports and brings power to our everyday realm and is the very same world into which the shaman-visionary journeys to bring back information, knowledge and healing.

A Way In

The way to access this realm is to first acknowledge the possibility of its existence and then to welcome communication with it. When we are open and hold an invitation then entry can be easy.

A good way in is to imagine this realm as the place of your true knowing and your higher or more attuned self.

The visionary quest continues in a way that allows an opening and a merging with the realm behind this one. You will possibly find that the operations with the realm of fae have already opened a door to this too!

The way that you will be exploring the animals and the archetypal support systems in your visionary quest is through four main entry points: Brain Opening and Mapping; Dreamtime; Journeying; and Archetypes on the Land.

You will be continuing to work with your intention. The idea will be that you give your intention over to the animal and archetypal supporting realm and then just allow imagery and experiences to evolve over the weeks.

Included is an opening to the messages in a Vision Council Meeting designed to bring insight and power.

Chapter 11

Brain Opening and Mapping

Focus: Opening Brain Powers

Setting Up the Earth Whisperer Brain Study

I would firstly like to talk a little bit about the human brain, to help you to see what is available to us in our brains that is not generally accessed! Maybe this will help us to expand our minds! I also hope that it can encourage a rebooting of our ancient, animal selves and bring our own animal into communication with the animal realms.

Right Brain versus Left Brain Functions

The human brain is divided into two cerebral hemispheres connected by the corpus callosum. This gives us right brain and left brain functions. The sides resemble each other, but the functions of each side are distinctly different.

Scientists continue to explore how some cognitive functions tend to be dominated by one side or the other, that is, how they are lateralized. The left side of our brain controls the right side of your body and vice versa. Different parts of the brain control different functions of the body.

Brain anatomy is interesting. We know that there are specific differences in the two sides. For example, the lateral sulcus is generally longer in the left hemisphere than in the right hemisphere. However, we don't always see any functional differences. If a specific area of the brain is injured its functions sometimes can be assumed by another area of the brain.

Some Brain theories!

In 1981, Roger Sperry won a Nobel Prize for his "split brain" experiments. A patient who suffered from uncontrollable seizures had his corpus callosum removed through surgery in an attempt to control his illness. After the surgery the patient seemed to function normally, as he could walk, talk and eat. However, some astounding results arose. Tests were conducted individually on both sides of his body and found that his right eye and hand could name an object such as a pencil but could not explain what it was used for. The left eye and hand couldn't name it, but the hand could demonstrate how to use it.

According to Roger Sperry, "The main theme to emerge . . . is that there appear to be two modes of thinking, verbal and nonverbal, represented rather separately in left and right hemispheres respectively and that our education system, as well as science in general, tends to neglect the nonverbal form of intellect. What it comes down to is that modern society discriminates against the right hemisphere."[7]

Isn't this interesting? Our society is a mould that stops our right hemispheres from working in their imaginative, non-verbal and whatever is beyond this (possibly an opening to the mythical and other planes) way. The drivers in our systems keep us compromised. Perhaps there is a listening, opening and reconnecting preference waiting to be switched on in us.

Paul MacLean developed the famous Triune brain theory, which was very influential in the 1960s.[8] MacLean's original model distinguished three different brains that appeared successively during human evolution. Over the years since, several elements of this model have had to be revised, but it is a useful model for understanding how we are wired. The three brains are the reptilian brain, the limbic brain and the neocortex.

The reptilian brain is the oldest of the three and first appeared in fish, nearly five hundred million years ago, then continued to develop in amphibians and reached its most advanced stage in reptiles, roughly two hundred and fifty million years ago. It controls the body's vital functions such as heart rate, breathing, body temperature and balance. Our reptilian brain includes the main structures found in a reptile's brain (hence the name): the brainstem and the cerebellum. The reptilian brain is reliable but also tends to be rigid and compulsive.

---

7 R. W. Sperry, "Cerebral Organization And Behavior", *Science* 133 (3466): 1749–1757. doi:10.1126/science.133.3466.1749.

8 P. D. MacLean, *The Triune Brain In Evolution* (New York: Plenum Press, 1990).

The limbic brain emerged in the first mammals, about one hundred and fifty million years ago. It can record memories of behaviours that produced agreeable and disagreeable experiences and so it is responsible for what in human beings are called emotions. The main structures of the limbic brain are the hippocampus, the amygdala and the hypothalamus. The limbic brain is the seat of the value judgements that we make, often unconsciously, that exert a strong influence on our behaviour.

Lastly, the neocortex began its spectacular expansion in primates, scarcely two or three million years ago, as the genus Homo emerged. It culminated in the human brain with its two large cerebral hemispheres that play such a dominant role. These hemispheres have been responsible for the development of human language, abstract thought, imagination and consciousness. The neocortex is flexible and has almost infinite learning abilities. The neocortex is also what has enabled human cultures to develop.

These three parts of the brain do not operate independently of one another. They have established numerous interconnections through which they influence one another.

Setting Up the Earth Whisperer Practice

Let's use our brain now to make up a fun activity with it! I have tried this exercise a few times now and it never ceases to blow my mind how this exercise recalibrates my way of thinking. Prepare for new perspectives!

☙

EXERCISE
Brain Attunement

This week your task is to attune to the two hemispheres of your brain and then the three brains, and allow each of them to take you on a Visionary Quest of about fifteen minutes. The quest can be anywhere—a walk in nature or a time in your home or garden.

Remind yourself of your intention for this book. Follow this intention in some way as you allow each part of your brain to lead the short quests below.

Prepare for your Visionary Quest with your left hemisphere, right hemisphere, reptilian brain, limbic brain and then the neocortex. The way to do this is simply to tune in to your whole brain and thank it for its amazing existence within you! Then pick up a rattle and focus on the part of your brain you will be working with today or in the exercise. As you rattle, allow your consciousness within this part of your brain to awaken. Acknowledge it with your wider consciousness and ask it to let you get to know it. See what colours, images, senses, impressions, feelings and shapes come to mind. Perhaps this part of your brain will appear with a separate guide.

After ten minutes or so of rattling and inviting the consciousness to come to the fore, set out on a short journey outdoors or through your home. Alternatively, you might also choose to do a Visionary Quest by sitting and allowing this part of you to lead an artwork creation, drawing, piece of writing or composition of music with an instrument or through bodily sounds like clapping, humming or singing. Let this part of your brain really have permission to hold the show. After about fifteen minutes (or more if you need more time) come back to the everyday, allowing the brain part in focus to come back into balance with the rest.

Make notes of your findings!

Chapter 12

Dreamtime

Focus: Entering Dreamscapes

In dreams we experience the visionary world. Everything is alive and connected. Animals can speak with us. Our ancestors can travel vast distances to meet with us. We journey into other realms. We shift spaces as if by magic. Our dreams preserve for us the magic that one day we may bring into our everyday lives too.

The word for shaman or healer in the Mohawk language is *Ratetshents*. The word literally means dreamer. In this tradition, dreams are said to reveal the "secret wishes of the soul". The daily task of the community is to gather around the dreamer, help them recognize what the soul is saying, and then take action to honour the soul's purpose.

Imagine if we had this practice alive in our communities again!

Setting Up the Earth Whisperer Practice

I often use the fact that we dream in our sleep every day as an encouragement for those who are looking to open up to the other realms and be able to journey or vision-walk. What I say is this work is innate to us every living day of our lives when we are asleep. We just need to allow ourselves to relax, much like we do when we sleep!

When we sleep our brain waves slow down in exactly the same way as they do when we drum, rattle and go into shamanic trance opening to visions.

We come out of our everyday beta pace to a slower alpha then delta and even slower theta pulse.

This week you will be working with your dreams to invite the realm behind this one and the animal archetypes and deities to come and communicate with us.

EXERCISE

Animal Dream

Before you go to sleep, take a set of animal cards or ask for a certain animal to come into your mind. It might be an animal that you are seeing often in your life or it might come from just allowing space in your mind for an animal to come to consciousness. Have a clear picture of this animal and then, in your awake state, spend some time having a conversation with it. Ask the animal if it will bring you some information about the intention you hold for this Act and your life at the moment.

Keep a pad and pen next to your bed.

See what your dreams or your waking thoughts bring. Sometimes people have immediate results with this. Often it takes a few weeks. You might find that the answers come at some point over the following day. Be open-minded and supportive with yourself. This work has a timing and way of its own!

Take notes and at the end of your time focusing on this task bring together a summary of your experiences and ideas.

Chapter 13

Journeying

Focus: The Power of the Drum

Earth Whisperer Drum Study

The first known historical record of a drummer of either sex is of Lipaushiu, a Sumerian priestess who lived around 3000 BC. The earliest drum was recorded in a painting in Catal Huyuk in the fourth century BC. Drummers and animals together are often recorded, especially the bull, holding the vital image of the female reproductive organs and equally perhaps representing male virility and power.

Frame drums are the traditional instrument of visionary practice and seem to have emerged into different parts of Europe from Egypt and Greece. The Ancient Egyptians also used the metal jangling instrument the sistrum. The use of the frame drum is known in ceremonies to support manifestation and also to summon the certain return of life after winter. The painting of drums in red, later to be buried with their drummer at death, is an important ritual conveying the drum's essential role of ensuring that the realms beyond this one can be connected with, woven into and operate as an essential companion and playmate with this world.

In the Greek tale of Ariadne, Ariadne supports Theseus to overcome the bull or Minotaur (death/ego) and emerge from the labyrinth (initiation) in order to undergo a rite of passage and achieve enlightenment. Ariadne is seen as the one with the thread, or as the bearer and beater of the frame drum. Her beat faithfully sends the pulse of the spiritual power through to Theseus that he may come through the ordeal with success and transformation and that the Minotaur may progress to the other realms and then perhaps be a messenger for Theseus.

The power of the drum to invoke the opening of veils to allow the animal archetypes and their corresponding deities to come through and communicate with us is immense.

Setting Up the Earth Whisperer Practice

In the Earth Whisperer practice with drumming, you will be knocking gently on the drum's membrane and the threshold between worlds, to see which animal archetype is waiting to meet and share wisdom with you.

✦

EXERCISE

Drumming

We are going to find out about some of the deities of certain traditions and their counterpart animal archetypes.

Your task in this section will be to read through the list and see who interests or holds meaning for you.

Wear your Protector, setting the intention to only connect with what is true and right for you in the following exercise.

For three days, set yourself the task to drum with your intention and any question that may come to mind from holding your intention. Your question may also be an intention for healing. For example: "Bring me courage and strength so that I can feel ready for this" or "Let me receive whatever healing will support me in the accomplishment of my intention." Allow an animal to emerge in your vision. Who has come through for you?

Then allow yourself to merge with this animal and drum as if you are it. Feel into how it is to be this creature in its archetypal form. What does the animal want to convey to you? Be open to listen and sense deeply. What does it want you to be able to access for it? Why has it come to you? What is resonant or profound about your relationship with this animal spirit? How is it to be in its energy field? When you put out for healing, what is the medicine that this animal brings through?

Keep this relationship through merging and drumming for about ten minutes and then thank the animal and detach. Write some notes. Now go walking for twenty minutes with the animal spirit with you and see what happens. Know that you can call on the animal to walk with you at any time and that you can ask for it to stand between you and other situations whenever you feel you would benefit from its presence and its power to match and remind your own to come through.

What happens on the walk? Do you see the world or your life in a different way?

Some of the Hindu deities with their animal archetypes:

Sun God Surya: **Horse**

Fire God Agni: **Ram**

Creation God Brahma: **Swan**

War Goddess Durga: **Lion**

Purifying God Ganesha: **Mouse**

God of rain Indra: **Elephant**

War God Kartikeya: **Peacock**

Fortune Goddess Lakshmi: **Owl**

Knowledge Goddess Saraswati: **Swan**

Protector God Shani: **Crow/ Raven/Vulture**

Fertility Goddess Shashti: **Cat**

Health Goddess Shitala: **Donkey**

Destroyer God Shiva: **Bull**

Preserver God Vishnu: **Eagle**

Lord of Death Yama: **Male Buffalo**

Loyal God Ayyappa: **Tiger**

Vayu (the Wind God): **Horse**

Varuna (the Water God): **Crocodile**

The river Goddess Yamuna: **Tortoise**

Bhairava, a manifestation of Shiva: **Dog**

Some of the Egyptian deities with their animal archetypes:

Aker: **Lion**

Ammit, the Soul Eater: **Lion/ Hippopotamus/Crocodile**

Anti: **Falcon**

Anubis: **African Golden Wolf** (formerly **Jackal**)

Apophis: **Serpent**

Apis: **The Mighty Bull**

Ash: **Lion/Vulture/Hawk/Snake**

Babi: **Baboon**

Banebdjedet: **Ram**

Bast: **Cat**

Bennu Grey: **Heron**

Hathor: **Cow**

Hatmehit: **Fish**

Hedetet: **Scorpion**

Horus: **Falcon**

Khepri: **Scarab Beetle**

Mafdet: **The Wily Mongoose**

Meretseger: **Cobra**

Nekhbet: **Vulture**

Sekhmet: **Lioness**

Seth: **Aardvark/Donkey/Jackal/ Fox**

Sobek: **Crocodile**

Taweret: **Hippopotamus**

Thoth: **Ibis/Baboon**

Unut: **Hare**

Chapter 14

Archetypes on the Land

Focus: Meeting the Archetypes in the Landscape

In this final practice of Act 1, the focus is on meeting the archetypes in the landscape and allowing ourselves to be empowered by and open to the healing stories that the land we live on provides every day.

Landscape Study

A first way of meeting the archetype in the landscape is through an Earth Whisperer practice I call "Story divining". A second way is by bringing members of a well-known myth on journeys with you, either outdoors or around your home, and being open to messages they give to you. I call this Earth Whisperer practice "Story Companionship".

Here is a story that I have worked with a lot over the years. It is the Scottish story of Bride and Angus and is called "The Coming of Angus". It basically tells the story of the archetypal openings and initiations of winter moving through to spring. It is a theatre of the landscape of Earthly life that informs and holds us as humans and the one that draws out the archetypal battles, learnings and growth that we experience in this human realm. Each archetype can then be medicine for strength or for meaning, understanding and hope when we allow ourselves to study with them or become close with them. The Earth Whisperer Landscape exercise following the story gives an example of how to do this.

Read the story below and ponder on what makes an impression and what it leaves you with. Take some notes.

The Coming of Angus and Bride

Summer was surrendering to autumn. Nature's colours were turning from green to orange, red and brown. The blustery wind was blowing the leaves to the ground. Beira, the Cailleach, Queen of Winter, was looking serious as she wandered back to her cave in the mountains. She swept the cave with her broom and prepared it anew for the dark nights of winter that would eventually arrive. It was time to work hard to ensure there were plentiful supplies for the dark season when she would take her place as ruler over this Domain. By spring she would have to return to the Green Isle and drink from the Well of Youth at dawn, before any bird visited the well or any dog barked in the morning light. Then she would sleep until she awoke again refreshed and young. In summer she would become a woman and then by autumn again she would age to be an old wrinkled hag, ready to take her reign once more as the fierce Queen of Winter. And so this is the story of time.

The Cailleach liked her time of winter rule. She had heard a prophesy that spring would only come again when Bride, the green maiden, came into the land and married the Cailleach's son, Angus Og. Beira had other wishes and wanted to prolong her time of reign to forever if she could. So Beira sent out a search until Bride was found. Beira bound Bride in ropes and carried her back to her cave to keep her captive for the winter.

Once in the cave Bride was a prisoner. She was forced to work menial and difficult tasks. Beira continually criticized all that she did. Bride was permitted to venture outside the cave but only as far as Beira's magic would allow. Beira gave her a daily task: to wash a black fleece in the burn until it was white. No matter how often Bride washed the fleece, of course it would not change to white. Bride was miserable and she longed for warmth, spring and to be free. That day seemed like it would never come. Resigned to the tasks she was given, Bride spent the days of autumn and early winter going about her daily chores with a sense of structure and purpose. Despite the Cailleach's intention to weaken her fugitive, Bride grew stronger and more skilled.

Meanwhile, beneath an oak tree on the Green Isle Angus Og, the Ever-Young, slept deeply through much of the winter. In the depths of his hibernation, he had a recurring dream. In the dream, he met a young maiden dressed in green, and hand-in-hand they walked through a forest full of blossom with fairy folk in procession behind them. As they walked the woman was silently sobbing. When Angus awoke he knew that these visions were not just dreams, but actually visions of something he was meant to remember. He went to the King of the Green Isle, Mannanan Mac Lir, to discover the portent of the dream.

"Who you have seen is Bride, weeping because she is kept prisoner by Beira, your mother. Your mother fears for her reign because she knows that when you meet you will be married. This will bring on the summer and you will instead reign as King with Bride as your Queen."

"Then I will find her and free her from Beira."

"The winter is at its height now, you would not get far. Wait until Beira begins to weaken."

Angus tried to wait, but every night he was traumatized by visions of Bride and her weeping. It was too much for him. So again he approached the King of the Green Isle.

"I must go and find Bride before these dreams drive me crazy." Angus spoke with determination.

"The wolf-month (February)is here now," the king said. "The temper of the wolf is too uncertain. You must wait."

"I cannot, it is time for me to go. I will borrow three days from August and use them here so that I may begin my search."

So it was that Angus used his magical fairy skills to bring three days from summer and place them in February. He rode across Scotland searching for Bride. But the Cailleach's cave was hidden well. She couldn't be found.

It was in those days that Bride went to the pool in the burn with the black fleece to wash it in the water. The water was freezing cold and it numbed her hands, turning them red. She wept in hopelessness at the insanity of this task.

As her tears fell into the burn an old man with a long white beard came up the glen. He asked her, "Who are you and why do you weep?"

*"I am Bride," she replied, "and I am held captive here by Beira
the Queen of Winter. Every day I have to wash this black fleece
until it turns to white but it never changes, I am so fed up of these
ridiculous tasks."*

*The old man reached out and took the fleece from Bride. He
shook it three times and on the third time it turned white as
snow. Bride stared in bewilderment. He then reached down and
picked three white flowers, snowdrops that were suddenly growing
between them, and handed them to Bride.*

*"Take the fleece and these flowers to Beira," the old man said.
"Tell her that they are beginning to grow in the woods, tell her the
first sprouts of grass are appearing on the edge of the woodland,
and the cress is appearing along the burn."*

Bride was astonished. "Who are you?" she asked.

*"I am Old Man Winter. I am on my journey north. I take the
frost with me, except that which Beira holds fast to."*

He turned away and continued on his journey up the glen.

*With happiness, Bride ran to the Cailleach's cave to show her
the fleece. But the Cailleach paid no heed to the fleece and stared
at the flowers in Bride's hand.*

"Where did you get those?" she cried, her voice filled with horror.

*"They are growing in the woods. Grass sprouts in the field. Cress
grows along the burn," Bride replied as instructed by the Old Man.*

*In fury the Cailleach took up her black hammer, the one that
she used to pound upon the ground to bring frost. She called upon
her hags, the ones who were mounted upon shaggy goats and who
brought the winter winds and storms with them. They rode across
the land spreading the frost, with the fiercest of winter storms
howling in their wake.*

*These storms drove Angus back to the Green Isle. Whenever
the winds receded, Angus would again return and search for
Bride. Those who saw him spoke of Angus's return. Even the birds
carried word of Angus across the land. In time Beira heard that
her son was again in Scotland and her rage called in storm after
storm, which drove Angus away.*

*Despite the conditions, Angus continued to search. Until one
day he found her. It was in birch woodland a distance from the
Cailleach's cave. Her hold on Bride had lessened as more and*

more of her energy went into the perpetuating of winter. Bride could wander further away.

When Angus and Bride took each other's hands, the forest came alive with the songs of birds. Immediately, the ground opened before them and there emerged a procession of the fairies, who led Bride and Angus down into the hall of the Fairy Queen and King. They married and their togetherness took the vibrancy of youth through the land. The growth of the green world came into the world again and the ice and frost began to melt.

Beira felt the change and knew that Angus had found Bride. Again she cracked her hammer to the ground to increase the frost and called upon her hags on their shaggy goats to bring wind and storms across the land. The sudden chill sent a shock across the land. Fairy folk fled back to their homes and the fairy palace closed up again. Angus and Bride found themselves alone in the forest. They mounted Angus's white steed and rode back to the Green Isle before the Cailleach could catch them. On the Green Isle they would be safe and could spend their days in ease away from Beira's torment.

But absolutely nothing would appease the anger of the Cailleach. She roared across the land bringing cold and storm wherever she went, determined to stop spring from ending her reign.

Beira used her power to call upon three storms. The first was called "The Whistle" and it blew high and shrill, bringing with it a chill wind and hailstones. It drove the people inside and killed the livestock.

Next she called upon the "Sharp-billed Wind", which pierced and pecked at everything like the sharp bill of a bird. There was nowhere to hide from this storm, so intrusive was it.

Next, she called upon "The Sweeper". This was a fierce winter gale that swept across the land and took down everything in its path. It tore down trees and ripped the roofs off houses. Many perished in these storms and with the famine that followed many young animals died.

The land was so ravaged. This brought great pity to the heart of Angus Og and he knew he had to return to the land to try to help. He prepared himself for battle. First he faced the hags on their shaggy goats, who sought to drive him back with wind and storm. Angus persevered and fought the hags, eventually succeeding in driving them away to the north.

Beira was alarmed and enraged, but it was not over yet! In the laws of magic she knew that she had the card to play of the three days of winter, as Angus had snatched three days of summer when first searching for Bride. With her own magic, she unbound them and set them loose upon Scotland. Angus fled back to the Green Isle, fearing for his life. In those three bitter days so much harm was done.

By now the Cailleach was greatly weakened. She had not the strength left to fight or prolong her reign any more. She watched as Angus and Bride rode back onto the land. In surrender, Beira made her way to the Green Isle, throwing her hammer beneath the holly tree as she went.

On the day of Beltane, in the early dawn, the Cailleach drank from the waters of the Well of Youth, before any bird visited or any dog barked. She fell into a deep sleep. Angus Og and Bride took their rightful place as the King and Queen of summer.

︿ ﹀ ︿

Setting Up the Earth Whisperer Practice

After reading this story of the dramas of the land, it's time to step into the nature landscape in our everyday lives. After divining stories for ourselves, we will take a walk with some story symbols!

EXERCISE

Archetypal Landscape Meeting

Part 1—"Story Divining"

Story divining happens simply by being open to meet the archetypal landscape around us. It happens when we set the intention of meeting everything in our world on an archetypal and meaningful level. This honouring that everything is looking to interact and meet us with meaningful messages all of the time is a great truth. Often when I am holding workshops, the messages and omens from the world around me are heightened because I am completely focused on being in a multidimensional state of heightened awareness. Every turning, song, exchange, conversation or appearance in the world around the workshop is extremely profound. Taking time to work with this and note it brings even more meaning and merging.

For this exercise, after becoming present and clearing your mind, set off on a walk. You will also be holding true the intention you have made for Calling and for what you need or are curious about right now. Take a notepad, camera or your phone with you for recording. Prepare to be able to collect lists and impressions of meaningful imagery, signs and members of the Earth community you might encounter along the way. Make sure you hang out and pause at places that might call you to linger longer. If you are walking in a town or city, look for numbers, words, snatches of conversation and juxtapositions.

When you come home with what you have found (perhaps after half an hour or an hour) here is the task: Concoct a story, poem or picture from what you have collected.

What did this exercise allow you to access or realize?

⌣

Part 2—"Story Companionship"
Again become present. Choose one of the archetypal characters or significant symbols (for example the fleece, the hags, snowdrops) of the story of the coming of Bride and Angus to take as a companion on your walk.

As you walk with them, ask them questions and their opinions, just as you would a friend.

When you return make some notes on what you learnt and experienced from this exercise of "Story Companionship" and your entering into the story field of the wider story in your local landscape.

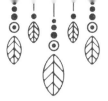

Scene 5: Reflecting

Consolidating and Receiving

Here we are at the end of Act 1! We can now take some time to think about and honour the calling in nature and the calling in the archetypal worlds. At the end of this journey, know that the energy is deep for divining.

Have a look back through your notes for Calling. Write down what you sense you are now moving on from. Have a look at what you have written and consider this. Now draw a line underneath what you have written.

You may also choose to take your intention and tick off what is changed in you or what has now been allowed. Take the time also to feel into what is yet to come. You can make a fire if you wish and feel the opening to completion and then the readiness for the new. When you go to sleep at the end of this reflection, ask your dreams on this night to bring through power for the calling in the new.

On the next morning, if you can, awake to watch the rising of the sun. As it rises, or as the sky grows lighter, feel all of the members of this Earth community you have connected with in Act 1 with you. Feel all the members of those in the realms behind this one with you as well. Feel all the dimensions possible that you have invited to be a part of your experience, there in their own way.

Make a sign, sing a song and pick up your drum to make some beats that convey gratitude, honour and appreciation for all of them, while also honouring and appreciating yourself. Feel how far you have come in this time.

Ask who is there for you in the new.

See who is with you.

Honour the calling in everything.

As you drum, vision a world where the calling in everything and the way that everything interacts, communicates and holds relationship together can be accessed and valued. Be open to receive.

Make a wish.

The curtains close on Act 1. It is time for an interval.

Ice cream anyone?

With Calling behind us, Act 2 is ready to begin.
So, now we will navigate the great adventure of time!
We are about to open up the timelines of past, present
and future. Here you can feel your place as part of an
empowered continuum. We open doors and reconnect
with parts of our soul that have lain dormant or hidden.
Get ready for some potential great findings!

Act 2

Loop

^ ⌄ ^

A Circle of Inclusion

Loop is a time-traveller Act that holds a power to open the
dimensions and see ourselves beyond the everyday. We travel in
a loop. We enter the loop through present times. Then we open to
an exploration of the realm of the past and the ancestors. Next we enter
into the zone of the vision of the future ones and ultimately back to the
beginning of time. In Loop, there is the possibility to powerfully connect
with what it is to be a visionary engineer and step out of the confines of
what we imagine time to be. There is also the chance to bring healing
for ancestral issues and traumas that may have haunted us for years.
Loop assists us to examine our ideas about future. It searches our souls
to catch and relieve burdens or hopelessness that may be affecting our
contemporary lives and the lives of the ones who will come after us.

As you are taken through to the time continuum of Loop, you will
find yourself coached by nature and presence. There is an additional aim:
to understand, clear and transform blocks and difficulties in operating
in each of the three time zones of past, present and future.

Shall we begin?

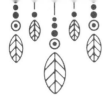

Scene 1: Prep Aligning with Loop

I often travel back to the beginning of time. In my imagination I go there. I just travel, simply, like a child at play, and sit in that silent place of potential.

Perhaps you do this consciously too? I expect we all congregate there when we meditate or feel absorbed in a task, complete in the sense of oneness with everything. Do you know the great void? Do you ever enter that incredible place in between here and other places? It can also be experienced as the great death. These are the places where we encounter silence and the Holy Communion with what is. I know that when people I am close to die I am suddenly swept to this place. It is the experiences that have happened during these moments that have ripped me out of inherited belief systems and led me on this quest to try to map and understand what is really the true geography of this life.

The beginning of time is accessible whenever we go to a place of non-attachment to the forms our eyes see and brains habitually register. The beginning of time is accessed through the realm of imagination.

Imagination

Imagination refers to the faculty of the mind that forms and manipulates images. The roots of the word "imagination" are with the mid-fourteenth-century Old French word *imaginación,* which means a concept, mental picture or hallucination. In Latin, it comes from *imago,* meaning an image or a likeness.

Did you realize that the word imagination has the root of magic—"magh"—in it?

Magic

Magic is a late-fourteenth-century word, *magike.* It means the art of influencing or predicting events and producing marvels using hidden natural forces. The word "magic" links to the Old Persian word *magush,* which is possibly from the Proto-Indo-European root "magh-", which means to be able, have power.

An Imagined World

Can you tune in to how everything is imagined really? Can you feel how "magh: to be able; to have power" is what we are all born with? Can you see how the constructs around how we place this power and this imagination define how we live our lives and place ourselves?

I wonder if you can reflect a little on what those constructs for you are in how you position your imagination? Do you take imagination seriously enough and value it? Do any of us?

I am an artist. Imagination is my playground. I believe that we are all artists and that the role of this visionary work I play with is to help support everyone to tap back in to this. I find my place within the idea of being a team of modern-day visionaries working for the good of the future.

My calling has always been to take art back to its true place again. I have always known that the place of art is in the imaginary realms, feeling into the spirit of the times, learning with and harnessing the powers of creation to bring an effect into the current lived reality. As an artist, I wanted to learn how to map this place so that I could free art from its political holding. Who would have thought that the spiritual practice of being with what is and holding presence with the body and the breath would be the state I would find that would bring us to be able to access this place of potential that is also the beginning of time?

The beginning of time is accessible to children whenever they enter the energy of play. So, naturally it is also enterable by adults when we remember we can all play this way! The potential at this juncture is a power that is reachable all of the time. This power is a place of co-creation and the potential that will bring support to any situation. It is the power of wholeness that was "all that was" before this great fragmentation of everything began and it has never gone away. It is the power of wholeness that exists all of the time when we step out of the convincing illusion of separation.

Ah, the confusing illusion of separation! Duality is the existence we are apparently born into and then born out of again when we die. The scripts of duality are incredible experiences of the many facets of what could possibly be a part of this wholeness. This story we live in is a way to experience the many facets. Our lives are such a gift to come closer to the great mystery. Yet we forget the wholeness and so are imprisoned here.

I wonder if you can spend a moment now imagining the part of you that can access this space of wholeness and potential alongside the part of you that lives in a state of duality?

When I tune in in this way, I begin to see how there is a part of me that can tap into this vat of potential and imagination all of the time. The other part of me is living what has been imagined!

I wonder if you can spend a moment now feeling into what might have imagined your life?

Freaky isn't it? If you do this regularly, you get to see that there are many threads that have imagined us! In order to gain back my power (the meaning of "magh", remember) then I need to click that all that has imagined my life is a part of me and I am not separate from this. Then I can join in and get on with the task of imagining an unconditionally loving world of creation where everything has power to express and be itself together.

My understanding is that my early ancestors knew how to access this great place of potential all of the time. The evidence of archaeology points to there being a time (Paleolithic and before) when there were no weapons or fear of being taken over. When I travel back to meet the early people, I always meet them attuned to the expression of the planet and especially the local environment. I also feel them connected with the archetypal realms behind the one we live.

The evidence of archaeology also shows the existence of places on the Earth's surface where this place of potential could be accessed more easily than at others. My remembering in my soul is that I have always known how to enter this place and I have always known how to time-travel. I periodically interact with myself in different times and places, weaving with some kind of time-travelling project. My experience of place is that the ancestors there can always be reached and that the voices of the future ones are not only calling us on, but also the inspiration for everything we do today.

Which Way Does Time Go?

When I was pregnant with my son in 1999, I rented a room in a town close to the country cottage renovation project I was working on with his dad, just until the cottage was ready. On the landing outside my bedroom was a poster. On it were these words:

Treat the Earth well. It was not given to you by your parents,
it was loaned to you by your children.
We do not inherit the Earth from our Ancestors,
we borrow it from our Children.
~ Native Proverb ~

With my first child in my belly, of course the sentiment of these words and the synchronicity of the message being outside my door at this time had a profound impression on me. Time seemed to go backwards from what I had previously felt when looked at this way. Becoming a mother, my whole concept of time shifted. The caravan of creation apparently ran back *to* source not *from* it! This blew my mind! Over the years I began to comprehend that actually either way you went it was the same source. Suddenly, one day it became apparent to me that this was the mystery of death! Everything was one big Loop, often experienced as cycles.

Why Time-Travel?

The truth is that some of us are, and always have been conscious time travellers. I remember at the peak of an initiation when my children were at the *Doctor Who*-watching age, looking forward to *Doctor Who* night with all my heart and thinking that this time-travelling eccentric truly was the one who could understand my soul. I remember a particular episode when the Doctor's assistant, Rose, became the mind of the Tardis. She could see into everything. I recall thinking that I knew just how she felt. The mirror was startling. Yet it also shattered the illusion that I was ever going to "fit back into" ordinary life in the same way I had before my significant initiatory opening when my grandmother had died. On a visionary journey, when we initiate, time and its dimensions can open up to us big time. It is never possible to fit back into the human body and social patterning in the same way again. We have to go through a period of adjusting ourselves to an awareness that we are living in this time and in other times also. Eventually there can be integration. This usually comes through a search to understand what has happened and a deep surrender to a path that seems to guide us to where we need to be led to learn about what is happening. In time we are able to put the right filters and actions in place to be able to commit to a life in many worlds.

In this case, the time travel is less of a choice and more of an inevitability.

Then, there are others who seem to be able to walk more sure-footed in the everyday world and time and yet who long to open these windows of the soul to reach the other times. They appear to manage a more graceful way of this initial happening. The opening of these windows may be through study, prayer, shamanic journeying, sign walking, intuition developing, writing and singing to the ancestors and the future ones. The more deliberate practices can open doors to these streams. I wonder which way your path has taken with this time-travelling ability? I wonder if you are aware of the extent of it?

Whatever the way, the longing by request or by default to sense what is beyond this time and space will lead an initiate to a profound encounter with the mysteries of creation and death.

What Does Initiate Mean?

To initiate is to enter the new and undiscovered. It is to make an initial. It is to enter an opening. To initiate is to undergo the cracking open of an old form and enter into a state of something not yet experienced. In the mystery schools of old, initiates would be the ones who were growing into their mystical knowing selves. The teacher is the initiation itself and the guide on the path is often someone who has an experience that means that they understand the way of initiation. An initiation is something that happens to take us on this journey. So as graceful as an opening to the other worlds and times might be, it is often the growing out of an old stage, the bereft territory of a life change or a death of a loved one that leads us to this place. Initiations have us traversing territories that can only be taken alone.

The World Is Flat. Oh No It's Not!

Remember how there was a time when the world was thought flat? Before that, the ancients knew the Earth was a sphere, as the mathematical stone circles and alignments show us well. But at some stage, the belief that the Earth was a flat plane returned. Well, that's how I think about the way we seem to think in these times. Time is a line. We can't go around it and we can't go backwards or forwards.

But honestly, let's challenge that belief. Really it can be a loop.

Reunion

Let's call the ethos of Loop a reunion.

Time travel is all about reunion. How often do you daydream and find yourself drifting back to times in your earlier life or into ideas of what might become? How often do you dream for yourself or for your loved ones? The act of recalling memories or dreaming into the future is an intimate relationship with longing. We long to connect and reconnect. We long for union. Reunion is our true nature.

When I learnt about shamanism, I was taught that the shaman was someone who interacted with spirit worlds through altered states of consciousness, such as trance. I was taught that the goal of this was usually to direct these spirits or spiritual energies into the physical world, for healing or other purposes. Our natural state is reunion. Whether our culture or our own choosing defines us as shamans, visionaries, soul-searchers, daydreamers or those who play, I believe we all long for union and the bringing together of a world that shows the truth about time travel again.

Ego and the Idea of Continuum

The ego, as named by Freud and later recontextualized by Jung, is a strong façade of ourselves we create in order to belong, be accepted by our tribe, and to keep ourselves safe. The ego learns to comply and behave in a way that is culturally acceptable and is built from not wanting to be punished or die. The "far out" idea of a continuum of time that we can access at all times could be a bit of a challenge for the ego as the ego prefers predictability and conformity.

I recommend finding a way to honour your ego and the part of you that numbs out, denies, laughs at or feels threatened by some of the things you begin to find out on this journey with Loop.

Get to know your ego and the way that it behaves and love it no matter what. The ego needs lots of compassion and gratitude for what it is trying to do. For in truth, the opening to a spiritual paradigm is ultimately the ego's death. Honour yourself, your ego every day and the ego in the world around you. However, don't worship it or give way to it. You might have to be quiet, lie low and just get gently on with your own way at times. You definitely will need to cultivate both a deeper humility and a strength of knowing. The exercises in the first three chapters will support you with this.

Allowing a Flow

Loop is a flow. It is a continuum. It is a circle with no beginning and no ending. It lets you go wherever you need to go. Remember through this time that allowing a flow also means that you can choose to pause wherever you are.

Become a Director of flow. Choose to be in charge of your own limits and choices. Trust that you know what you need, as well as knowing that things will change for you.

Visionary Practice

Here we revisit the map of the Visionary practice. The examples take you through the four concepts of nature, trust, knowing and presence again but this time you practise this with present, past and future timelines.

Presence and the Three Pillars

Presence
Presence *is the central pole of everything in this practice.*

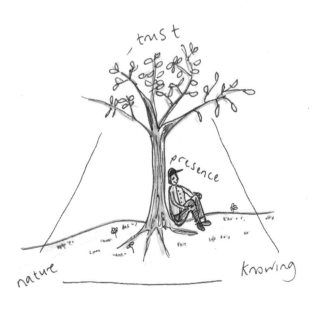

Nature
Nature is the first of the three pillars in the visionary model.

EXERCISE

Nature (with Presence)

The first thing I am going to ask you to do is to find a special place in nature with a tree, where you can sit regularly all through the next three months. It might be your garden or a tree on a walk close to you. Attune to where this place is going to be and resolve to dedicatedly visit this place for the duration of the course. Take about twenty minutes or more for this Being Concept task.

Go to your chosen place in nature. Sit with your back to the special tree that you will visit regularly. Take some time to become present. Focus on your breath and simply become mindful to what chatter inside your head might be going on. You don't need to push it out. Presence is about allowing awareness to arise and comes from a different place to the mind chatter.

Let yourself move into your senses. Touch—feel the air on your skin, touch the ground with your fingers and the surface of the tree, grass and nature around you. Smell—breathe in the scents. Taste—taste the air, lick the grass, bark, a flower. Hearing—let your ears take in the sounds. Sight—let your eyes cast on everything as if seeing for the first time. Let nature join you through your senses.

In this space, bring yourself to awareness of being present and in the moment. You are looking to become present with nature both within and without. Now imagine this presence as being able to exist throughout all times. Take yourself to the beginnings of everything. Feel the origins. Feel the today. Allow a conversation to happen, moving with presence with your senses and nature through these two stations of presence.

Bring yourself back. How do you feel about nature now? How do you feel about your own true nature and nature around you? Make some notes on how you found this experience.

EXERCISE

Nature (with Presence of Others)

Part 1—with Incarnated Humans

Now I invite you to feel yourself and all of us humans as being a part of nature!

Include trees and all of nature here!

Go outside. Spend some time walking mindfully. Be aware that you are a soul living in a body in a physical realm called Earth and that you are anchored in a time called the present. Take some time to register all the other members of this Earth community all about you. Feel the physicality of this plane we all exist in together. Deeply acknowledge every living part of nature you can see or might be there but you can't see them, in your world. Be aware of the other presences on this Earth plane like the trees, plants, sheep, rain, air and birds. Try to imagine or tune in to some of these other beings especially to try to feel how it would be for them to relate to this present-moment Earth plane too.

Now call to mind your current Earth family who live in this plane with you. Recall the members of your family who are alive and also any special significant others for you. Take some time to register what it is like to be in your body and how it feels to relate to this present-moment Earth plane.

After about ten minutes with this exercise, take some notes.

Part 2—with Ancestors

Include trees and all of nature here.

Open to the idea of the existence of the ancestors of the land you are on now as nature beings as well as human ancestors of the land and your own ancestors.

Deeply acknowledge every living part of nature that has lived on this Earth before this time. Be conscious of the other presences on this Earth plane in the past like the trees, plants, sheep, rain, air and birds. Try to imagine or tune in to some of these other beings especially to try to feel how it would have been for them to relate to this past-times Earth plane too.

Now do the same for the human ancestors of the land and for your own ancestors.

Imagine how your soul and your ancestral soul are connected. Feel a bubble of light all around you and your energetic body. Ask that a soul guide can hold your vibration clear and true for you. Set the intention that in this exercise you are kept clear and state that you are not available to take on any feelings of others in other times, but just to be open to acknowledge and honour everyone and everything.

Think about the existence of previous generations on the land you stand on right now and imagine how the soul of the land and these ancestors are connected. Connect with the idea of previously met trees and nature elements that have existed on this land too. Open up to the world of possibility that all of these different realms of soul can have a place here. Make a place for your ancestors and a place for the ancestors of the land. Feel how this present moment on the Earth plane and other planes of time and experience can exist together. Find a way to open up yourself to appreciate your own soul and the world around you as part of a wider soul though space and time.

What does this feel like?

Take the next five or ten minutes to honour or acknowledge your ancestral nature souls, the personal relative souls and the souls of the ancestors of the land where you are who have died and have passed beyond this time and space. You will be opening a special council space for them just by honouring them. You may do this through song, speaking aloud to them, gently ringing bells or leaving biodegradable offerings. Everyone senses in different ways, so be aware this may feel very subtle. The fact is if we reach out then what we reach out to can feel the invitation. Sometimes this takes lots of practice and the building up of a groove and relationship to be felt by you. Sometimes it can be felt very easily.

After you feel complete, thank everything and say goodbye for now. Close the space by asking the soul guide you connected with at the beginning to sweep between you and the soul of everything like a curtain that closes with respect but continues to honour in a different way. This will make sure you can go back into your everyday life and perception more smoothly and keep focus.

Take some notes on what this was like for you and what you perceived.

⌣

Part 3—with the Future Ones

Open to the idea of the existence of the future nature beings, including the future humans, of the land you are on now and your own family's future descendants through whatever branch they may continue. Imagine how your soul and your future ones' souls are connected. Feel a bubble of light all around you and your energetic body. Again, ask that a soul guide can hold your vibration clear and true for you. Set the intention that in this exercise you are kept clear and state that you are not available to take on any feelings of others in other times but just to be open to acknowledge and honour everyone and everything.

Think about the existence of future nature beings and future generations on the land you stand on right now and imagine how the soul of the land and these future ones are connected. Open up to the world of possibility that all of these different realms of soul can have a place here. Make a place for your future family descendants (if there will be any for you or for your siblings) through whatever branch they take. Make a place for the future ones of this land. Feel how this present moment on the Earth plane and other planes of time and experience can exist together. Find a way to open up yourself to appreciate your own soul and the world around you as part of a wider soul though space and time.

What does this feel like?

Take the next five or ten minutes to honour or acknowledge future family relative souls and the souls of the future nature ones and humans of the land where you are. Feel again how you are opening a special council space for them just by honouring them. Again, you may do this through song, speaking aloud to them, gently ringing bells or leaving biodegradable offerings.

When you feel complete, thank everything and say goodbye for now. Close the space by asking the soul guide you connected with at the beginning to sweep between you and the soul of everything like a curtain that closes with respect but continues to honour in a different way. This will make sure you can go back into your everyday life and perception more smoothly and keep focus.

Take some notes on what this was like for you and what you perceived.

Knowing

*When we think about a visionary or someone who sees or has "the sight" we are really connecting with the ability to know and are describing this as a way of truly seeing. This kind of sight goes beyond the way the eyes see and into the inner vision. It is this **knowing** and this development of inner vision and the ability to see to the heart of something that is the second of the three pillars in the visionary model.*

EXERCISE

Being Knowing

Part 1—Today

You will need a drum or rattle for this task.

Pick up your drum or rattle. Visualize a bubble of light around you that holds presence. Set the intention that you are only available here to connect with your knowing. Choose a colour to coat the bubble around you that sets the boundary that this is a clear space for you. You can extend a second bubble to go all around your home and the boundaries of the land around your home and set the same intention. Sit and connect with being present again.

Now focus on your knowing. Think of a time when you have known something. Begin to tap on a drum or shake a rattle. You can do this for about fifteen minutes. Connect with your knowing and let all your attention and the attention of the drumbeat flow to hold awareness for this knowing. Ask yourself, "Where does this knowing come from?" Feel the origins and authenticity of your knowing. Let it strengthen and take its place. Observe what happens for you.

(It is also possible to do this by playing a drumming track, but I highly recommend developing your relationship with presence through drumming and having your own drum.)

Come back and thank your drum and the space that held you. Take some notes.

⌣

Part 2—Ancestors
Repeat the above feeling into the space of the knowing of the ancestors through a caravan of time.

⌣

Part 3—Future Ones
Repeat the above feeling into the space of the knowing of the future ones through a caravan of time.

Trust
Trusting ourselves and developing the ability to discern is the third pillar of the visionary model. We will be holding presence for the development of this trust.

🍃

EXERCISE

Being Trust

Part 1—Today
Go back to your place in nature. Move into a place of presence again. Be in your senses. Take some time to land and be with the Earth and the weather. Feel yourself as a part of this wider system. Now open up to feeling the interconnectedness of everything. Become aware of the different systems within the outer nature that you sense are operating right now. Feel how

they work together and the plan that they are a part of. Feel into your trust for this plan.

Now feel all of the systems going on within you and your body, mind, emotions, passions. Feel your organs and your blood flow, the beating of your heart, your lungs breathing, your eyes and the way your thoughts respond to your eyes working. Feel how you connect with the outer world through your lungs and your sight and thoughts, your sense of smell and your emotions.

Move back again to your awareness of the systems in nature outside of you and the plan everything including you is a part of. Feel into your trust for this plan.

Spend about fifteen minutes in this being with trust. Come out of the task and then make some notes on how you found this and any insight you had.

⌣

Part 2—Ancestors
Repeat with trust of the ancestors.

⌣

Part 3—Future Ones
Repeat with trust of the future ones.

Setting an Intention

Now it is time to reacquaint yourself with intention. I wonder what your intention will be for Act 2? You may also choose to use a different one for Loop or work with the same one as in Calling. This will be referred back to throughout and is your personal satnav for this journey.

When you picked up this book what was it that you were feeling called to do or experience? Spend some time opening up whatever it is that is your desire.

Take some time to write down your intention for this initiatory adventure. Feel into it. What is important to you? What would you like to feel like or know better when you complete this journey? What is looking for healing or reconnection? How do you feel your pull to adventure?

Write this down and make a special board that you can pin your intention to or a box you can place inside. Now take some images to surround your intention with. These can be photos of places, people, ancestors, deities or animals that inspire you. If you choose a box, then you can place objects like special stones inside. The idea is that you are energizing your intention with things that you find powerful and supportive.

Now make a visit to a special tree or nature place. Whisper or speak your intention to connect with your calling and everything that goes with that to your tree. You may also choose to leave something with the tree that represents your pull to adventure, and place it inside an opening or hang it loosely from one of its branches.

The Adventure of Loop

The word "adventure" comes from the Latin root *adventurus,* which means a thing about to happen. It first appeared in English in the thirteenth century, in reference to something that happens by chance or by luck.

I am holding the intention that Loop will be an adventure. I have the idea that it will be a way into initiation that helps us to become more intimate and caring with the part of us that can sometimes struggle with the unknown.

What we are opening up to together is to learn to be a community of time travellers who feel safe and qualified to open up in the fields of time. I will offer many stories along the way that can make this journey reassuring and mapped well for you.

Most of all, I am trusting in the divine providence and benevolence that is overlooking each of our journeys and that operates in the way of chance and luck. Get ready for the most amazing surprises!

The Path Ahead

Here is an itinerary of what is to come!

Each time has a link with earth, air and then water. Fire is the passion you and all the ones in the loop are holding and works through you and everything. There is a link with a land animal, bird and sea animal and then a plant with the different environments and time stages.

Each of these chapters in the scenes will offer different aspects to consider. The plant spirit and spirit animal will bring perspective and medicine. There are tasks in each chapter that will help you to open up an adventure and to also equip you with some exciting healing work.

Preparation

Here are some things to collect to prepare for your time in Loop:

- Notebook
- Pens and pencils
- Art materials
- Sketchbook
- Drum
- Rattle
- Tambourine
- A selection of drumming or peaceful music tracks
- Smallish hoop made from willow or similar
- Bowl for water
- Camera
- Sound recorder
- Outdoor waterproof clothes

So, Scene 1 has been set. The curtains now open to Scene 2 and a contemplation of Present Lifetime.

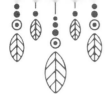

Scene 2: Present Lifetime

Spirit Animal Hedgehog and Plant Spirit Rose

Come into the present moment. Contemplate your life.

Take a seat. Here, sit down and take in what is around you and how it feels to be in your body in this lifetime you live inside.

Here in Present Lifetime in Loop, you find that the place of power is in the present moment and in yourself. You are the point of connection with everything. Because you are here and because you register that you are here while being aware that there are so many other points of time and space, you have the power to effect change and listen to the vision in everything. The present exists only because of our knowledge that past and future are there. This is the way that consciousness works. To be present is to be in relationship with the backdrop of memories of what was before and then the dreams of what is to become.

Protector

I love working with the idea and the spirit of a Protector. It helps me out so much to remember to connect with Protector energy. I call the Protector "that which holds the truth of who I am like no other". I feel the Protector as particularly strong because it is clear and it is like me. It holds a clear vibration of what is most true to me. That means I can't get lost or tend to lose my identity so easily.

Let's begin our work in Present Lifetime by connecting with a Protector that we can call the Time Protector. Let's connect with something that can be our base to return back to, a steady reliable compass or a reminder of who we are when we lose sight of our true selves and potentially get a bit entangled in time and space.

In this present moment that you have just been making an attempt to come into, see if you can focus on your breathing and let yourself come more and more into the present. Really be with the now in the room or the place where you are. Try saying, "present moment" as a mantra as you feel into the space and the awareness of who and where you are. Stay here for a couple of minutes acquainting yourself with the now.

Slowly now, can you bring your awareness to the memories of what was before this moment in time and the dreams of what is to become? Feel the past swerving as an ellipse behind you and then the present before you, swerving to meet the curve of the past. Can you perhaps begin to feel yourself as part of a big time hoop engaging with the memories and dreams of the vat that is yours and the memories and dreams of the vat that belongs with the collective? How does that feel? Now as you do this, can you come to appreciate the reality that you are powerful in all of this? How easy is it to get to this place of power?

Make yourself available now to tune in to the note in this big whirly collectiveness through time that is your note. Spend some time tuning in to this. You might feel the vibration of it in your heart, hear it in your inner ear or see the place it signals from in your mind's eye. Wait until you really feel that clear distinction of what is you. You have lived it all your life so it is possible that it could find its way to be distinguished quite easily once you make space for the rendezvous. Can you find a colour or a shape for your note? Can you find something that can represent what it is that is making your note? It might be a bird, a rock, a star, a bug or an animal of some kind.

This is your Time Protector that you have found! Take some time to get to know your Time Protector and ask some questions. Ask for a name. Try asking him, her, or them if you can feel it around your aura protecting you or if you can feel them going into some situation you find difficult with yourself. Ask questions on how this Time Protector can help strengthen and hold you through time. Ask any questions that feel important! There are adventures ahead together!

So we open up to the Present Lifetime initiatory adventure now and head out first onto land. We have hedgehog as an animal guide for this first part of our quest and we have rose as a supporting plant spirit.

Let's open the curtains to your current life!

Chapter 1

Land and Perspectives on Time

Chapter 1 opens the Initiatory adventure to explore the territory of your current lifetime. We focus on land and perspectives of time. We have hedgehog as our animal guide here and a few different concepts to consider on our journey. We look at nature time and man-made time. We explore our shape-shifter aptitude as humans and contemplate ego.

Working with Hedgehog

Hedgehog is a creature that lives very close to the Earth! It is also a creature that knows how to protect itself and one that can change form according to the energy needs of the time. It has between seven hundred and nine hundred spikes (or quills)! Hedgehog is often seen as a symbol of fertility and a sign that ideas and plans can prosper.

EXERCISE

Connecting with Hedgehog

Now over to you! Take yourself out onto the land to find a nature spot that you are attracted to that is particularly earthy for you. It might be by a group of rocks, a place in the woods or a sheltered earth-scented glade by a burn or stream. Let yourself come into a sense of connecting with the land and earth element here. You are preparing yourself to connect with hedgehog.

Tune in to hedgehog and intuitively ask it some questions. You are going to find out what earth means to hedgehog. Get ready to go deep into opening to hedgehog and the nature spot where you are and allow hedgehog to help you to even more deeply connect with what land and earth is about in present times. Hedgehog works in a way here that will bring you even more into the present through your engagement with the physical realm. Spend about ten minutes asking questions and taking notes.

Another way to do this task is to wear your Time Protector and then merge with hedgehog to receive information more easily by direct revelation. To do this, you simply feel hedgehog in front of you once you are wearing your Protector (it acts as a filter to keep you sovereign and clear). Ask hedgehog for permission to merge. Then pick up on information from hedgehog and ask questions. At the end of the exercise, detach and thank hedgehog, then rattle around yourself and detach from your Time Protector.

Take notes!

Kairos and Chronos

The ancient Greeks had two words for time: *chronos* and *kairos.*

Chronos refers to chronological or sequential time. Chronos is quantitative. He is the personification of time in pre-Socratic philosophy and later literature. He was depicted in Greco-Roman mosaics as a man turning the Zodiac Wheel and is usually portrayed as an old, wise man with a long, grey beard, similar to Father Time.

Kairos, on the other hand, signifies a proper or opportune time for action. He has a qualitative, permanent nature. Kairos is an Ancient Greek word meaning the right, critical, or opportune moment. Kairos also means weather in modern Greek.

Chronos is about measurement and ordering, whereas Kairos is about the feel of time, the magical fateful aspects of time, and has a deeper and nature-alluding way of operating.

My early supervisor Grant Clifford introduced me to these concepts years ago and ever since I have found them incredibly useful to map myself, my visionary nature and the often more quantitative world I seem to occupy. When we are working in the present moment, considering the forces at play through these two perspectives on time can be extremely helpful. Sometimes, it can be hard to work out if we are living on the same planet as everyone else! Often this is because of the simple Kairos and Chronos differences.

When I feel confused, I ask myself, "Which system am I working with here?" and remind myself that as a more visionary type I am generally a lot more in the Kairos than the Chronos. I find honouring both Kairos and Chronos as ways helps to ease the tension I can feel in the interactions I am a part of.

EXERCISE
Connecting with Kairos and Chronos

You will need to wear a watch or carry a clock or some kind of timetable that can represent Chronos for this exercise. Go out to your tree in nature, or any other tree that grabs your attention.

Ask the tree if you may sit with it and tune in. Feel the tree standing rooted behind you. Let yourself land so you are properly reminded that you are actually a part of nature in nature. With you and the tree in the same zone, come steadily into the present moment, becoming aware of all of the sounds and movements around you and allowing everything to just be.

Now tune in to "weather". Remember modern Greek calls weather "Kairos". Feel yourself in communication with the weather. Now ask to connect with the Kairos in the weather and spend some minutes attuning to Kairos. Then ask to open the Kairos within you. Bring them together. What happens?

Thank Kairos.

Now bring your awareness to your watch, clock or the timetable you have brought out with you. Tell the tree what time it is. Tune in to the clock face or the timetable and the workings of Chronos time. Tune in to all of the elements of the modern world that are driven by this measuring system. Now make space for all of the aspects of our world that help the measuring, like the sun, the moon cycles, the stars in the heavens, the standing stones on the land, the habitual patterns of the birds, insects and all creatures as they work with the times of day and with the seasons. Feel the great messenger service of the Chronos time that is in nature too. Now ask to connect to the Chronos within you. Bring them together. What happens?

Thank Chronos.

Make some notes on what you learnt about yourself and present time from moving through this piece of work. Who is Kairos to you? Who is Chronos? Who do you need to build a relationship with the most? Or are they both equal to you? Has anything surprised you about this piece of work?

Ego Safeties and Shape-Shifter Ability

We have explored the different perspectives on time as we live in this present lifetime. Now we are going to have a look at the different ways that the human manifests as a result of these perspectives. All of this will support you to understand what you are operating inside so that you will be a clearer signal and antenna for the vision of the times.

It's time for the ego and shape-shifter feature!

So, you know how I wrote in the introduction that the ego keeps us safe? The ego really likes to measure alongside Chronos. Chronos is often the ego's best friend. Sometimes it will unnecessarily manage and measure out of a previously built fear. When you look at it this way, you can begin to see how the world of Chronos and the clock has got so much anxiety in it!

Here's the other fact. Humans are the only being in the whole of nature who have the unique feature of being able to shape-shift into other forms. I mean, you might not see a person change physically, but inside, the ability to absorb, take on impressions and mimic the emotions and behaviours of others is super-advanced. Parrots copy words and chameleons change colour, but honestly, the human being unconsciously and famously likes to merge, shape-shift, change thought forms and have a party for the range of emotions of others most of the time!

Who are you really and who am I?

I love that we shape-shift so well. I love this absolute longing and inclination of the human being to merge and feel for others. I believe it is what gave us the role of being custodian and caretaker for the Earth. This ability enables the visionary, magician, the shaman, the actor and the empath in each of us. We are made to be able to deeply connect with others. Remember that reunion is our birthright and nature.

Unfortunately, for some reason it often isn't pointed out to us that this is what we do. One of the jobs we have in Present Lifetime is a cleaning-up operation. We enter this cleaning-up operation so we can help the ego to recover and not be so anxiety-driven. Another of our tasks is to have a look at the shape-shifter ability and find out how to free the visionary magician from the net of absorbed behaviours.

EXERCISE

Exploring Ego and Shapeshifter

You will engage more with the earlier task of cleaning up with your work with rose. In preparation for this, the invitation is to connect with ego and then to connect with shape-shifter as two what I will call "aptitudes".

Take three chairs or cushions. Place them in a triangle facing to the centre point. Name one "me", the second "ego" and the third "shape-shifter".

Sit in the place for "me" (meaning you!) Come to a place of connecting with presence, knowing and trust in the manner you are used to by now through the Visionary triangle.

Then sit in turn on the ego seat for five minutes and the shape-shifter seat for five minutes. Take notes in each of these spaces on how this feels and how you experience the ego and shape-shifter within yourself. Where do you feel each of them? What colours come to mind? Where do you go? What emotions do you feel? Is it easy to hold this station? Are either of these states familiar for you? Is one more familiar than the other? So you like what you are finding? You can complete your time on each cushion by visualizing a waterfall of light moving through you and the ego or the shape-shifter and cleansing and refreshing anything that came up for you. Take a good shower with the waterfall of light if you need to before you detach.

Thank the ego and shape-shifter parts of you for their gifts and for what they are showing you.

After you are complete, rattle around your body and return to "me".

How was this experience? Were you surprised by anything?

So now, you have connected with your Time Protector and know that you can align with them to centre yourself at any time. You have landed with hedgehog and felt a connection with the Earth in these times. You have seen how there are at least two different vantage points on time and are also beginning to establish a relationship with your inner ego and shape-shifter as they operate. From this protected, grounded and more time- and perception-aware place, we are ready to move into the next territory.

Chapter 2

Rose and Soul

Rose

Rose is a plant associated with beauty, love, protection and secrecy. The flower is used for rosewater and perfume and its scent is known to bring calm to the heart and nervous system. As a flower essence its application is for invoking natural power.

For years, I have worked with the rose flower spirits and a spirit-collective that understand the properties of rose for the shamanic unravelling work in my practice. I have no idea what they do! I just know that when I asked who could come in and support me with some of the deeper embedded issues of clearing and freeing, it was this rose collective who came forward with my grandmother's ancestral gypsy line and the results of what they administer together has been astonishing.

We are going to work with rose to do some cleansing work. But first of all we need to introduce the concept of soul.

Soul

The way that I have been shown soul is that it is the essence of being and is generally considered to be the eternal aspect that brings each us into life. Soul can move beyond the body to communicate with everything and is the part of us that holds trust and surrender to the way of things. Soul doesn't worry. But sometimes there are things that happen that can mean that we don't find it easy to connect with aspects of our soul. This can be through conditioning, birth trauma, difficult incidents and damaging relationships. Sometimes we can have a way of being that means we are sensitive to the world and need to build the personality and boundaries that can allow us to engage with life and be able to come back to centre.

Rose can bring healing to our connections with our soul from the effects of our current lifetime. It can also be an extra Protector for us—a Present

Lifetime Protector—in supporting us to stay connected to our own unique way. Think of those thorns!

EXERCISE

Opening Up Space and Senses and Setting the Dial

Here is an exercise for opening up space each day through our senses and a meditation that will bring cleansing and flow to your life.

I recommend you begin your days from now on with a space-opening exercise that is similar to what is described below. This will support you to be able to stay grounded in your life and to become more and more true to yourself, while allowing you to open up to feeling the present life in a more aware way. Being able to work with the dial that is introduced here will help you to remember that the everyday you who has an everyday role and place in the world needs to be able to function and move easily through life.

⌣

Daily Setting Space

Today I open up myself to clear vision. I see my soul able to flow and be free to show its own true rhythm, pathway and inclination. I set the intention that I can be guardian of this innate expression of soul and be responsible for my own inner listening. Meanwhile I will always endeavour to work in harmony with all the Earth by seeing the soul of all other life able to express truly too.

In this moment, I place myself as human as an authority of my human life and my needs. I imagine a dial in my chest. I know that I can turn this dial to low and to high, as I open up to connect with my timeless nature. At times, I will choose to turn the dial right down and simply live in the everyday and with what keeps me present and quiet and that is okay. At times, I will choose to open more, turning the dial up slightly. Knowing I am in charge of regulating will help me to move with this time-travelling project in a fun but not an overwhelming way.

I open up my soul to connect with the land and all of the special sites, beings and places on this land. I honour the ancestors of the land here. I honour the future ones of the land here. I honour all the beings, creatures and manifestations of nature that live here with me. I see the land and all of its places and beings being able to be felt, heard, seen and given audience and inclusion again by humans.

I open up my body to be able to connect with the true healthy energy of this amazing Earth I live as a part of. I set the intention that I can become more and more in alignment with the soul of the Earth and the true vibrant essence of the whole of this planet.

I open up my connection with the vibrant energy in my own living body. I feel my intent to be able to listen to and understand the way of my body and its simple needs. I know that by listening to my body and by accepting its limitations, knowing and boundaries in each moment I best serve myself and my life. I know that these needs and limitations can change at any time.

I connect with the energy of the personal vision I bring to my life at this moment and bring a space to mind now where I place this alongside and within the true potential vision of this planet. I feel both of these visions finding their place with the visions of myself and the Earth through different times of our evolution through past and future.

I acknowledge that in this moment I honour the power in myself and in everything to effect positive change for my life right now. I know that in this moment I am initiating a pathway for flow that can also affect other times and spaces in a positive way. I know that the pathway for flow is set at a gentle but true gauge so that the soul of myself, my family and my Earth community through all times can be settled and held.

EXERCISE

Rose Soul Protector

It would be great if you could find an actual rose bush to sit with for this exercise. If not, see if you can get a rose flower to have in a vase, or access some rose essential oil and smell its scent. If none of these are possible, then simply call on the spirit of rose to be with you.

Invocation of Rose

Choose some gentle music or a quiet and slow drumming track to play that lasts fifteen to twenty minutes.

Sit and bring yourself into the present moment, feeling your Time Protector holding space for you. You can imagine you are wearing your time Protector like a glove or cocoon for your whole body. Feel the holding.

Call in rose and the spirits that work with rose and ask them if you may work with them. Imagine rose ready to imbue you. If you are sitting with a rose bush or flower, then ask if you can make a deeper connection with it as a plant and a flower. Be open to the relationship field between you becoming stronger.

Now bring your attention to anything in your life at the moment where you feel a bit entangled or clogged up. Become aware of how you feel in your body when you remember this subject or situation. Let the space in your body where you sense this take the stage, remembering that the Time Protector is holding space for you to bring strength and grounding. You can visualize the tree you connect with in nature at your back if you feel you need more holding.

Invite rose to infiltrate your body and imagine it going into the entanglement you feel with this subject or situation. Invite its essence and scent to take compassion, love and protection to all the places of this story and cleanse your system of the trauma or confusion that is there. Listen to the music or drumming and feel yourself letting go. Know that rose will transmute to light anything that is needed and that the compassion and disentangling properties can take to the light anything that isn't yours to carry here.

When you feel complete, or after about fifteen minutes, you can detach from the situation and the feeling, thank rose and ask that rose is blessed. Feel a waterfall of light cleansing and completing the piece of work. Thank and detach from your Protector and tree if you called them.

How do you feel now? How is your inner vision? Take some notes.

You can repeat this exercise at any points when you feel you would like to feel clearer. And you can also work with rose as a soul Protector, to help you keep your own eternal thread of consciousness clear.

Please note, if it becomes clear to you that it is a different flower and plant to rose that you are to work with then go ahead! Follow your own guidance. Find the one that hits the note!

Chapter 3

Spirit of the Age

This evening, I went for a run while thinking of soul. There is a burn that runs alongside our garden that I stand in each morning after yoga. I listen to it and also connect with the spirit of the mountain it flows from. It is the Ochil range of mountains that stand behind us. Recently, I have also been researching the River Tay for a project I am a part of. For eight years I used to live by the Tay. I would open and close my curtains to her each morning. I was surprised to find that the source of the Tay was close to Oban on the west coast and to see the extent of the river's journey and its tributaries journey through the land, before it reaches sea.

The rain had been pouring before I went out. Puddles and springs flowing from the hills were everywhere. I came back with my thoughts of soul alive and strong. I felt cleansed and rejuvenated.

I remember I made an art piece years ago where I etched onto a metal plate a drawing of the water cycle, printed it onto a luggage label and then attached it to a solitary washing machine drum. It alluded to thinking about the bigger picture and cycles within the cycles. The water cycles and the weather spirits connected to them amaze me. The rivers and all of their veins and pathways seduce me. The sea astonishes me and the different creatures that live in it are a constant source of fascination. When I was a

little girl and took myself off to Sunday school, I won a prize and was given a book token to buy a book for a presentation ceremony. The book I chose and was presented with was called *Mermaids and Sea Monsters*. I think I have always felt more aware of the power of creation within water.

When I tune in to the network of water and the Earth's weather systems, it feels so easy to be connected to and to be a part of the incredible power of this planet. As you probably know, humans are compositionally around sixty per cent water. Water is a big part of our nature. Perhaps water is in on this longing to connect and bring-everything-together notion that is the inspiration for Loop?

Bert Hellinger, one of the source practitioners of constellation therapy and the idea that there is a knowing field, has some thoughts on soul. Here is a great sentence he writes: "The greater soul moves in only one direction and that is to bring into union that which has been made separate."[9] I wonder if when I am connecting to water and the weather like this, and feeling powerful, I am connecting with the greater soul that Hellinger is speaking of? The soul wants to reconnect with everything that has been cast invisible. What is more, like water, it flows through us all.

So, while I was out there running on this evening, asking the rivers if they could teach me about soul, what I came back with was the feeling of connection with all of the rivers running through this land. I also recalled that all of the early settlements were by rivers and just how much the waters really are the waters of life.

Human Community

The focus for this chapter is humans and present lifetime. After this, we are going to attune to the wider web of the whole of nature, but right now it is the human tribe we will be giving our attention to.

I am wondering if there is a correlation between the greater soul and the soul of the age? When I was studying art in Cardiff in the 1980s, I often thought about the term *zeitgeist,* or spirit of the age. This was because I noticed that a lot of the ideas I would have for art pieces and projects would later come through in the advertising industry a few months later. There

9 B. Hellinger, G. Weber and H. Beaumont, *Love's Hidden Symmetry* (Phoenix, AZ: Zeig, Tucker & Theisen Publishing, 2000).

was so much synchronicity with this. One day, a professor mentioned the *zeitgeist* in a lecture and I thought, "That is it! Something is going on in the collective. There is a communicating spirit within art!"

I began to type automatic writing on my typewriter, where I would interview the spirit of art and invite the spirit of art to write letters to the people. I presented these as art pieces. Nobody was really interested in spirit in the political scene of 1980s British art and those ideas didn't really get out there, but they later sailed me out of the art world and into shamanism as an arena that gave them credibility and meaning. My aim has always been to free the spirit of art and to see that art is something that brings human community together and that speaks of the rivers of time.

Anyway, that is lots of stories about my path and me! The river is flowing. I want to bring the attention to you now and to your stories and to see the river flow for you.

Let's revisit initiation.

Initiation and the Vision of the Times

Remember how initiation was introduced in the beginning? To initiate, I wrote, was "to undergo the cracking open of an old form and enter into a state of something not yet experienced".

My daughter asked me yesterday if I found writing hard work. Really, writing is an initiation for me! The reason for this is because a lot of the time I am "winging it". I never actually know what I am going to write about. Writing for me is like the surprise I write of above of finding how far and wide the River Tay is flowing! Yet what I find when I crack something open is that I find my feet inside a greater vision and realize that I actually remember something that has always been there but has been unrealized. Writing for me is one of the best ways of channelling spirit and forging pathways. And to answer my daughter's question, sometimes it is extremely pressurizing and difficult, but if I make enough space in my life to be in nature and to love my life, it can be pleasurable.

I honestly think one of the biggest reasons why the majority of the Western world today finds initiation so gruelling is because we have forgotten how to put nature and our relationship with love and care first. I am sure that is one of the reasons why rose came through to assist in this course: we always have the reminder to wake up and smell the roses!

That is not to underestimate the difficulty of initiations and to say that finding them excruciating is a failure. I spent seventeen years in an excruciating one and when I fall down one of my wells into the next uncovering it is like another version of hell. But I do know that if I have self-care, allowing of myself and focus on connection with nature, then I can survive the journey with some special moments until I come back once more into the light.

Initiation is a cycle of time. Each year, lifetime, moon cycle, relationship, friendship or rite of passage is a cycle. We are forever turning. And within each of these cycles is an adventure with the elements. The spirit of the age is achieved through initiation. We have to birth the spirit of the age through what we go through and with the poignancy and meaning of our stories in their own right.

In the exercise below, we are going to connect with the initiation of these times and the cycle we are going to work with is the water cycle.

EXERCISE

Working with the Water Cycles

For the first two exercises you will either need to find a flowing river to sit beside, or turn on a tap. You will also need to take a notepad and pen or some drawing materials with you.

Go to a river or burn and ask it if you can connect with it. Say hello. Feel the water in you honouring the water of the river. Feel where the burn flows to and also from where it is flowing. Become aware that this particular water flow is a part of a complex system of rivers, streams and rivulets that flow both above land and below ground and that eventually will flow to the sea.

Now ask the river to connect you with the water cycles. Connect with rain, clouds, sun, heat, rainbows, thunder, wind, storms, mountain and sea. Feel yourself open to be any of these elements on the journey of the water cycle.

Now bring your thoughts to this current time in your life. What initiation are you currently going through? What is currently bursting open for you or stuck? What old form seems to be dismantling and leaving you in a place of the unknown? Or is there any longing in you that is buried that you are holding tight on to that is ready to reveal itself and start a flow? Does your intention for Loop speak of an initiation in any way? Take some time to let something rise to the surface in you, while in the field of the water cycle we have invited to hold space for us. Notice how you feel in your body and how your mind and emotions respond to this being given space.

Pick up the pen and paper or art materials that you have brought with you. Allow a story or some creative movements to flow that are latent in you. If you feel stuck for a starting point you can begin with the words or the thought, "One day, I listened in a new way. And this is what I heard." You may also choose to sing, dance or move in another way and record yourself on your phone. If you do this make sure you are on flat land away from the river so you are safe. This activity can put you deep into trance.

Thank the river and the water cycle when you are complete. Put away what you have written or created to look at later.

🍃

EXERCISE

Connecting to the Greater Force of Water

Connect to the river and to the water cycle in the same way. At the point that you connected to all of the different elements of the water cycle in the last exercise, go a step further and rest with the greater force that is behind all of this movement. Try journeying with the sounds of the river as a way to help you open up to this. Once you are there, stay with this force until you can feel yourself aligned with it, like a bird on the current of the winds perhaps.

As you connect to the greater force, ask for a story or some creative movements to flow that are about the collective soul initiation of the times. What are the possibilities of the vision that will be born because of this collective soul initiation? Again write or use your art materials or record a song, dance or movements.

As you come to a completion, ask the force to bring you information on your individual gifts. What vision do you hold for these times? What is your place in the loop from your present vantage point? Journey again with the river sounds as your music.

After this exercise, give yourself time to properly come back into the present moment. Sit with some trees and read through or look at what you have created. Make some extra notes. What have you learnt or reached from this time with the river and the water cycle?

Leave some offerings like hair, seeds, a song for the river, the water cycle and the spirit of the place. Wear your Protector and feel your feet rooting with the Earth. You can go back home renewed!

Chapter 4

Nature's Eternal Knowing

Don't you just adore thinking about the mysteries of creation? One of my favourite books is Layne Redmond's *When the Drummers Were Women*. I particularly love the sections in this book that link percussion to the fields of barley, wheat, corn and other crops from which bread are made. Layne writes about the magical practice of baking bread from the winnowing of the crops, the grinding of the flour, the rising of the dough and the heat of the oven that brings the dough to be a light fluffy edible loaf. She links this cycle with the dance of the feminine and the masculine, the god and the goddess, and with the eternal cycle of the gift that is life through manifestation on the physical planes and beyond the veils of death.

Early practices of singing, dancing, music and art were an act of communication with the cosmos as an opening to the source of life as it manifests. The ancients knew that we were a part of a much bigger map of realms and they knew how to keep the channels of communication open. They were confident that by doing this they ensured harmony and positive energy on Earth. It is interesting that the artefacts of this period were all in a time before weapons of war came into being! I have seen in my journeys how the ancients were communicating with the vision and the spirit in everything. Being human was very much thought of as being a tiny fractal along with every other communication of beings on this planet and beyond.

Here is a song I used to sing when I was young as a skipping game. I reckon the stamping feet and clapping hands used to be the frame drummers and dancers with their riddles and their instruments and that they were firstly women and then both men and women.

Oats and beans and barley grow.
Oats and beans and barley grow,
Oats and beans and barley grow,
You or I or anyone know how oats and beans and barley grow.

First the farmer plants the seeds,
Stands up tall and takes his ease,
Stamps his feet and claps his hands,
And turns around to view his lands.
Oats and beans and barley grow,
Oats and beans and barley grow,
Do you or I or anyone know how oats and beans and barley grow?

Then the farmer watches the ground,
Watches the sun shine all around,
Stamps his feet and claps his hands,
And turns around to view his lands.
Oats and beans and barley grow,
Oats and beans and barley grow,
Do you or I or anyone know how oats and beans and barley grow?[10]

∧ ⌄ ∧

So, now we are going to work with the mysteries of creation and set up a piece of work with the frame drum and a crop to connect deeply with a nature guide who will support you to return to your nature self. There is an opening of the portal and a ceremony to begin our travel through time.

Returning to the Nature Community

If it is August, the crops in the fields will most likely be ripe! If you don't have fields near you then either travel out to a field or sit with a bag of barley or corn flour, or get by some other means some sheaves that you can hold. You will also need a frame drum, riddle (a garden tool) or a tambourine. If it is not harvest time, then see if you can work with wheat, oats or

---

10 Anon: listed in J. Cushing, *The Fifer's Companion Containing Instructions For Playing The Fife.* (Salem: Cushing & Appleton, 1805).

barley flour or other milled produce and hold it in your hand or have it in a bowl in front of you.

One of the most powerfully transformative experiences I ever had was when my daughter and I were making corn dollies from barley grass growing in a field behind our house to give to people who were coming along for a trance dance. A lot in my life changed and I attribute it to the heady experience of working directly with the crop and an old tradition.

EXERCISE

Engaging with the Mysteries of Creation

Wear your Time Protector in the usual way.

Be in a field of a crop and put your hands out to touch the plant. If you are not local to farmland, hold a sheaf or flour from a crop in your hands. Tune in and ask that you can connect with the mysteries of creation through the plant that brings us bread and food and that has strong connection with the sun.

Now pick up the tambourine, riddle or frame drum.

Ask the plant to bring you a rhythm that you can tap out with one hand while holding the tambourine or frame drum with the other. Don't use a drumstick for this. Hand connection will make the practice stronger for you.

Let the tune come through and ask to be taken to the goddess and god that are synonymous with the crop you are working with. Once you meet them ask them to show you the mysteries of creation. Stay in this journey, tapping the riddle, drum or tambourine with your fingers and hand, for about ten minutes.

Ask the goddess or god of the crop if they would be a Nature guide for you over the coming months. If they suggest a different guide then get to know them and ask why they are to be your Nature guide.

When you come back from the journey, thank everything you have seen and felt and leave an offering with the land. Make some notes.

Opening the Portal

There are places on the Earth's surface that have been portals for time travel for millennia. Some of the most obvious are stone circles and church altars that are built on the crossing of leys, energy lines on the Earth's surface that work much like the meridians and chakras in our bodies. The ancients knew that connecting with these leys and especially their crossing points allowed an easier opening to the many realms of existence.

However, many are hidden. The one that I accidentally discovered, and that was most instrumental for me, was when I lived in Forres in the north of Scotland when my children were young. It was on the High Street, close to the library, and I found that when I walked through this area I would be aware of different times operating alongside this one. Journeying back into the experience later, I was able to map a lot about the experiences my soul has undergone in different times.

&

EXERCISE

Opening the Portal

Part 1—Preparation

Put on a drumming track or a piece of music that you can easily journey with, or pick up a drum or rattle. Make a journey to the nature guide you connected with in the previous task. Ask them to take you to a local place that's easily accessible to you on the Earth's surface that will be a portal for you in the work you will do. If they take you to a place that is impossible to travel to weekly, thank them for showing you and make the intention to energetically connect to this place in your portal task too. Keep asking them to show you somewhere local. Don't be surprised if it is somewhere like the tree at the bottom of your garden or a place you have been going to for years.

As prep, you are going to find out as much as you can about this portal place. Bring in your rose (or other plant) soul Protector and ask how to keep safe and grounded when you visit and work with this spot. Ask your nature guide to show you what the vision for this portal is in these times and what the vision is for you connecting with it in these times. It is no accident that you live where you live right now and that this portal is close to you. Why have you been brought together? What is the meaning of this new relationship in your story?

Ask for a ceremony to perform to open this portal and to honour its existence.

Ask for an opening connection sign and a closing connection sign to make so that you can enter and exit the portal with authority. Ask what to do to make sure you stay in the present while travelling too.

Lastly, ask your rose guides to go to this portal and to cleanse and clear it so that it is clear and safe for you to work with it when you visit. Watch them go there and trust that this will happen.

Thank your guides and this place. Come back and take notes.

⌣

Part 2—Visiting the Portal

Make a visit to the place you have been shown. Wear your Time Protector and your Soul Protector. Ask permission to work with this site. You will automatically be given permission if your nature guide has shown you this place, but it is polite and respectful to ask.

Find five stones and place them around this space so that they can be the four directions of the compass and the centre. Take your rattle and move to stand with the centre stone and feel a ring of light around you where the compass points move through. East as air, South as fire, West as water and North as earth. Acknowledge that your body and this Earth exist with the intelligent energy and cooperation of each of these elements. Now whistle and rattle to call in each direction. You are opening up a relationship with and acknowledging the presence and utter importance of the four elements in your life. Now feel yourself in the centre and whistle and rattle to acknowledge all of the different dimensions that operate that you opened up a connection to last week in the creativity wheel. Notice how you feel this in your body and how it feels in your circle.

Open space in this way or in a way that you are guided every time you visit.

Step out of the wheel and notice how you feel now.

Set up the ceremony as you were shown in the journey you made in Part 1 of this exercise. Remember you can enter and exit the portal with the signs you were given. You can also choose to exit the portal and be grounded in the now at any time. Journey with your nature guide as a guide and make sure you check in with them at all times.

If you feel nervous about this task, then you can work remotely from your home until you build confidence in connecting and disconnecting, entering and exiting.

Take some time to stand or sit and rattle or hum as you honour this place and all of its abilities. Sense the portal opening on the land through to the distant ancestors who had an eternal connection with nature and then through to the distant future ones who also hold this connection.

At the end of your journey, thank everything, stamp your feet, rattle all around you and feel the waterfall of light cleansing you. Come back to the present and take some notes.

Present Time Reflections

So here we are at the end of our exploration of the adventure of Present time.

Bring out the intention you have brought to Loop to look at again. How is your intention feeling so far? Is there anything you would like to change or adjust in the intention from what you have found out?

One of the intentions of beginning in Present time has been to grow more aware of the different filters that operate and that influence your openness to exploration. Ego and shape-shifter were introduced so you could become aware of how they influence you so you can take more risks and also be safe to do this. Focusing on soul and the idea that we are always operating in tandem with the eternal has hopefully brought in the concept that we are not entering anything that we haven't always been living with!

Looking at initiation as an integral part of growth and experience, and mapping with the idea that there is a collective spirit of the age that we are each individually in a wave with, will hopefully support our understanding in journeying with the past and the future that all time frames have themes and influence and can be answers and questions to other time frames on a continuum.

Including ourselves with nature helps us to open up to the greater story of our Earth and to set our own intention against the nature story that is happening as the theatre of today. You have a nature guide and a connection to a plant that will bring you more and more into alignment with your nature self each time you work with them.

You have your Time Protector, you have your daily opening of space with the vision calling central and you have the hedgehog and the rose as grounding and cleansing fellow Earth beings to connect with and find ease and clarity through at any time. You now also have a portal that you can work with over the next months for time travel.

In these next weeks, as you begin your time travelling, every day you will be pledging to come back to the present time and the vision of now. This is where your soul is housed from this perspective. It is natural you will be pulled to a longing to stay in certain times. I remember years ago, when I was time travelling a lot, feeling more of a sense of belonging in other lifetimes I would find myself in. My guiding spirit said to me, "It is what you do here that counts." It helped a lot to hear this. What counts is what is truly effective. Think of yourself like an engineer and that the place of power is today.

If you get attached to other times and communities, bring yourself back to the present and to nature here and back to your intention. Try saying, Robin Hood style (through Bryan Adams), "Everything I do, I do it for you." Nurture your love affair with the time you are identified in NOW and the calling that brought you onto this course! Call back the remembering of connection, joy, meaning and love that you find elsewhere to even more be here in this lifetime. See what you do as great soul restoration work for the planet and our lifetime. Invite the love you find in other times to be the passion behind everything that you set out to accomplish in the healing story that you are a part of today.

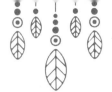

Scene 3: Ancestral Pathways

We have spent the first scene in Loop tuning in to present times and anchoring ourselves with the vision that is calling today. I invite you to appreciate this place of the present moment and the power that you have here in this time before we begin our time travel. Notice how you are feeling in your body right now. Notice how your senses relate to the world around you. How are you feeling about the prospect of moving to different stations in time? Are you excited? Is there a sense of wariness or worry going on in you? What does the past evoke for you? What does the thought of future evoke? Is one of these directions for time travel a more attractive prospect than the other? Make some notes about how you feel.

At this present fulcrum point in the great loop of time, let us cast our gaze now over our shoulders to bring focus to the ancestors. First of all, the human ancestors. There they are—the forebears. Can you trace a vine from you and your current family to those who are our recent relatives right back to the ancient ones? These are the ancestors who have paved the way for today. Imagine this: that everything these people dreamt of, thought, said, did, put their attention to or avoided created a path that culminated in what we live now. Who are these influential ones and how do you relate to them?

Let's consider the ancestors of the whole nature realm on Earth now. Think about this planet and all of the different landscapes that would pre-date today. What is it like to imagine these landscapes in the place where you reside right now? Think of another place you know and imagine the landscapes that preceded today there too. Perhaps you can begin to get a sense of that spirit of the age we were looking at in Present times in times gone by. What has taken place on these lands? Who lived here and what were the people and nature beings of the lands concerned with?

The house where I currently live is called The Bothy. This is its name because in times gone by it was a bothy for people who worked in the brewery that stood next to it. I often think of all the different workers who would have moved through the main part of our house and wonder at the parties that would have gone on here. I also feel a sense of something that is an ancient burial site that goes way beyond the age of this building. When

I tune in I get a lot of connection to a certain tribe who settled here and some of their spiritual traditions. I used to rent a gallery in another town that was the old Poor House for the church across the road. It was also part of a masonic building. There was the masonic emblem across the lintel of the door of the house next to it. Again, I had a real sense of the life and the spiritual traditions with the land that pre-dated my time there. Perhaps you live in a building with a history to it that you are already sensing, or have a sense that the land where you live has some story buried deep in the foundations?

This is the scene when we will be travelling to meet the ancestors and opening to feel more of a connection with them. We will be meeting them as a resource, as a place of wisdom and a source of great understanding and resonance. We will also be keying in with them to visit some places in their lives that may have directly affected your life today. With this in mind, we will be working with the animal and plant spirits of this direction to help bring healing and a new flow.

As we open the door to begin to meet the ancestors, the element, spirit animal and plant spirit for this section are introduced.

Chapter 5

Introduction to Ancestors

Element: Sky

In Ancestors, the element of focus is sky (or air). I am inspired to bring in sky due to the song below that I heard when I was beginning to assemble the material for Loop.

"Sky World"

*Skennikonhra Tewaton tanon iethiiehiarak ne ronatohetston
(skun nee goon law- dewadoon- dawnoon- yeh tea yeh
hyaw luck- neh- low naw doe hits doon)
Let's put our minds together as one and remember
those who have passed on*

*Teiethinonweraton ne akwekon skennen skennen akenhak
(de yeh tea noon we law doon- neh- aw gweh
goon- skun nun- skun nun- aw gun huk)
We give thanks that they are living in peace*

*Ne karonhiakeronon
(Ne- gaw loon hyaw geh low noon)
In the sky where they live*

*Io ha io ha io ho we ia
Ha na io ha io ho we ia
Skennen akenhak ne karonhiakeronon
(skun nun- aw gun huk- ne- gaw loon hyaw geh low noon)
Living in peace in the Sky World*

Let's put our minds together as one
And remember those who have passed on to the sky world
Their life duties are complete they are living peacefully
In the sky world, in the sky world
They will never be forgotten, no more pain, no more suffering
In the Sky World, in the Sky World.

Ha io ho we iaa
Ha na io ho we ia he
Io ha io ha io ho we ia
Ha na io ho we ia he
Ha io ha io ho we ia
Ha na io haioho we ia
Iooho we ia
We ha na io ho we ia he

Their life duties are complete
They are living peacefully
In the Sky World
In the Sky World [11]

---

[11] Theresa "Bear" Fox, "In the Sky World" (2005: Mohawk translation aided by Kaweienonni Cook-Peters).

Connecting to the Sky Element

Take a walk into the great outdoors! Lie facing up to the sky.
Allow your gaze to wander up, up, up through the air and the
sky. Perhaps a bird comes to greet you to be your companion
on this journey. Keep on going upwards and visualize yourself
entering into the ones who you can imagine are living in peace
in the sky world as in the song. Ask them if you may enter for
a few minutes. Close your eyes and visit them. Spend some
time with them absorbing their peace, power and dreams.

Spirit Animal: Vulture

In this book, vulture epitomizes honouring for us. When we honour, we
acknowledge and bring our respect, appreciation and kindness to something. A noble connection is made with what we are honouring and this
will energetically support a system.

Vulture first came to me when I was creating the material for Revival, an
advanced visionary course I led in 2014 that was about exploring the spaces
in between and opening up portals through time. Vulture came through
as Vulture Woman with the information that she was a helper of entering
the place between life and death and wouldn't run away from anything!

There are many varieties of vulture. Vulture is a species that is a large
bird of prey with the head and neck practically bare of feathers. It feeds
chiefly on carrion and so has the reputation of gathering with others in
anticipation of the death of a sick or injured animal or person.

In the ancient practice of a Tibetan sky burial, the corpse of a deceased
person is taken to a mountaintop to be eaten by birds of prey, most
commonly vultures. This tradition among some Tibetans, which is a
sustainable burial method, symbolizes the impermanence of life.

In the hieroglyphics of Ancient Egypt the vulture is the symbol for
the letter "A". Sacred and protected by the Pharaohs, it was known as the
"Pharaoh's chicken". Anyone who killed the Egyptian vulture would be
sentenced to death.

There is a story that the Egyptians believed vultures were female only
and that they were born without the intervention of males, by parthe-
nogenesis. This is why vultures symbolized purity and motherhood, but
also the eternal cycle of death and rebirth. Their ability to transform the

"death" they feed on (carrion and waste) into life elevates them. They were also distinguished by their supreme elegance in flight.

∧ ∨ ∧

As we journey with the ancestors over these next few weeks, we will really have the opportunity to appreciate just how important honouring is. We will see how if something or someone is missed, overlooked, rejected, forbidden or badly treated, then the impact can be severe for the descendants who follow. Honouring our ancestors, including and allowing all of their stories can be one of the most beneficial practices for opening a flow of life force for us in the present and releasing attachments to what is calling to be included in the ancestral storylines.

Vulture's power to "stay with" and not turn her back can be a big support in taking us to the places in our ancestry that have a lot of fear or guilt attached to them. I have seen my vulture guide fly me to the most forsaken of places to bring compassion and deep honouring where it is long overdue. It has always been well received.

EXERCISE

Visiting Vulture

Put on a drumming track, or pick up your drum or tambourine. You are going to visit vulture!

Make a connection with your Protector from Present Time. Then visualize yourself going on a journey across the lands to a place where you can find a tree with Vulture perched in it.

Ask Vulture if you can ask her some questions about what her role is. Ask her also about the importance of honouring.

See if Vulture can give you some information about how you can practise honouring in your everyday life. Ask her how you can honour the ancestors. Enquire if she can show you a ritual or short ceremony that you can perform each day to honour the ancestors. You can also ask if there is something that you can do at the portal place you have found on the land to honour the ancestors there too.

Connect with rose. Ask Vulture if she would be willing to take you on a journey to a place in your ancestry that is needing honouring. Ask her to equip you with whatever is needed to take to this place to honour them and carry rose with you. Ask her to come down from the tree so you can carefully climb onto her back. As she takes flight, feel yourselves moving gracefully through the air to arrive at the special place.

Call in all of the guides that connect with rose as soon as you arrive. Feel the balm and healing of rose working immediately. Keeping yourself held by your Protector, honour the ancestors in the way that you have been shown by Vulture. When it is clear that they have been truly honoured and that rose and the rose guides have thoroughly brought healing to this place that needs honouring, leave a special symbol in this place and then climb once again onto Vulture's back. Experience the flight of return to the place of the original tree with Vulture. Climbing from Vulture's back, thank her and leave her a gift of gratitude before she flies back onto the branch on her tree. Slowly come back to an awareness of the room you are in and return to the present moment.

How was that experience for you? Take some notes.

Honouring All of the Ancestors

Fern is one of the most ancient of plant species on this planet. As such its ancestral lines can take us way back! We are going to work with fern to set up a simple ceremony honouring all of our ancestors. This will be groundwork for the investigatory, connective work we will do with the portal and material in the next part.

Plant Spirit: Fern

Fern can be found all over the world. It is the most ancient of plants, along with mosses. The Earth began its life about four and a half billion years ago and fern probably began to live here about three hundred and sixty million years ago—that is two hundred million years before the first dinosaur! Surprisingly, ferns have branches like any other modern plants we see nowadays. It must have been the main source of nutrients for herbivore dinosaurs.

Ferns have unique characteristics in their physical appearance. Their stems and leaves are shaped like ostrich feathers and can curl up. It seems they evolved to adapt to the environment. Because of this physical evolution, they are one of the greatest and the most ancient survivors on Earth, living through the meteor crash that killed the dinosaurs and the extreme temperature of ancient global warming and the ice age. Wow!

EXERCISE
Attuning to Fern

We are now going to connect with fern and do a bit of serious time travel! First you will need to find a place in nature where there are ferns and where you will be unlikely to be interrupted. Maybe take a rattle with you to help you to tune in. Or perhaps just stand or sit with the fern, holding its leaves in one of your hands.

You might also choose to ask if you can take some of the fern back to your home and work with it there instead.

Connect with your Protector guide. Acknowledge the land where you are standing, and include in your scanning the present landscape and inhabitants and the past landscape and inhabitants.

Tune in with fern and ask fern to take you through its ancestral lines right back to the beginning of its habitation on this planet. Imagine a trail right back through time. As you go travel, rattle, sing or gently hum to let the vibration of your voice or movement honour the land, the times and all of the ancestors, including human and all of the many aspects of nature. Treat this task as laying a carpet of honouring with fern, from today right through to very ancient lands and times.

When you reach the origins of fern on this planet about 360 million years ago, ask if you can receive a message from fern from then to bring back. Spend some time tuning in to hear fern's whisperings, then gently drift back, holding the treasure of this in your mind and heart, to present time. Whisper your message directly back to fern today!

Take some time to make some notes.

Our time to work with the portal on the land you have made earlier has now begun!

Chapter 6

Safe Practice

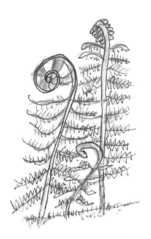

From now on, we will be working with the portal place that you prepared to work with in week four. Remember to always wear your Time Protector and your Soul Protector and to courteously ask permission to work with this site each time you visit.

Here is the procedure (or something similar you are guided to do) for each time you open up a piece of work here.

Remember the five stones that you have placed around this space so that they can be the four directions of the compass and the centre. Take your rattle and move to stand with the centre stone each time you work here. Remember to feel a ring of light around you where the compass points move through: East as air, South as fire, West as water and North as earth. Acknowledge that your body and this Earth exist with the intelligent energy and cooperation of each of these elements. Whistle and rattle to call in each direction. You are opening up a relationship with and acknowledging the presence and utter importance of the four elements in your life. Now feel yourself in the centre and whistle and rattle to acknowledge all of the different dimensions that operate that you opened up a connection

146

to last week in the creativity wheel. Notice how you feel this in your body and how it feels to be in your circle. Feel how you are utterly held and that you are kept clear and aligned.

Now, feel an orb of light around you and the space you are working in. Feel this meeting the four directions and then the central axis that holds all of the different dimensions. This will go up to the sky and down into the Earth. Imagine this orb as being about twenty-four feet in diameter. Feel the central axis just in front of you. Now set an intention that you are only available to connect with what is pertinent to what you bring as an intention each time. I am setting this intention with you.

Now feel the presence of spirits of the land and guides who will take anything that is attracted to this space to places on the Earth's surface close by where they can receive healing. Know that you don't even need to be aware of anything that might come close because these guides are so on it!

An extra bit to do is to connect with fern. Can you remember the message that you brought back from the original fern way back in time? Connect straight back with the place where you were given this message and then retrace that carpet that you felt laid journeying back to that time all those millions of years ago and feel the carpet connecting with fern and the unbroken lineage through to today. Call on the spirit of fern to hold space for you as you journey now to the beginnings of human activity on this planet.

Meeting the First Human Ancestors

Do you ever think about the first people? I think about them a lot. I wonder what they would have been open to without all of the types of conditioning we have today. Sometimes when I am in nature I feel like I can touch them as they exist in another time right next to me and when I am writing I often feel one of them inspiring and chugging me on my way. I have always been attracted to the standing stones of old and even though I know ancient people pre-date them, it feels like they mark clear existence as steady pointers towards a way of life that is interconnected and real in a way that I have been de-conditioned to have as a default.

Remember the quest of adventure that Loop signals to? Put on your time-travel clothes and pick up your tools. We are off to meet the first people.

147

EXERCISE

Meeting the First Human Ancestors

Years ago, I had a project working with some people, going to different places in Fife and helping to clear the fields of trauma in villages, hamlets and special places. This is not a project to clear collective trauma! That would be overwhelming for someone working alone. This project is to just work with your own individual story and anything that connects with allowing your intention for Loop to flow. So, when you visit your portal and take part in the exercises below, you will only be connecting with what is appropriate for you. Your rose guides have already been to the spot to set things up for you. You have your blanket of unbroken lineage with fern (you can also see this like a flying carpet that can fly you back home at any time!) and you have a way of setting up space so you can keep a clear focus at all times.

So when you are standing here at your portal place now, or connecting to your portal place from the clear space you have at home (which will be set up with the directions and the present moment in the same way) reiterate that you are only available to connect with what is clear and true for you and your personal part to play in all of this. Pick up a rattle, a drum or some bells to shake or tap and to open up the journey you are about to make into the past.

Feel the fern carpet beneath your feet and connect to your soul with your soul guide. See yourself now as the same unbroken lineage that is fern. Your soul has always been available for a visionary life. Your soul only knows the way of connectivity and intercommunication. Ask fern to walk you back now to the place where human life began on this planet. Feel your human soul longing to more consciously reconnect with the ancient human soul. Remember you have always been connected to this, because you couldn't be a part of this unless you were a part of the origins of this whole creative story of life. Feel the human and all of nature ancestors carry you back on this caravan of life along the fern carpet. Keep going and ask to be taken back to the birth of human consciousness. When you get there, simply drum or rattle softly and sing to them or be in the silence with them. Stay here for about ten minutes. Ask them if they can intuit a message to you to bring back to now.

When your ten minutes (of this time) are complete with them, change the tempo and bring yourself back again along the caravan of human and nature life and the carpet of fern. Stamp your feet. Shake your body. Move places and fully make sure you return. Thank everyone who supported your journey. Leave something with this place (e.g. scratching with a twig into the earth, making a symbol with parts of nature) that relays the message you were given to bring back to today. Hold what has returned as a message in a sacred place in your heart.

Knots, Holes, Karma and the Power of Awareness and Acknowledgment

In Gestalt therapy, a modality introduced in the 1940s and 50s, it is seen that any information that presents itself as emotive or difficult to integrate in the current times is information about something that has been brushed over and is needing to be seen from some time in the past.

When I first began to work with clients for shamanic sessions I would be taken to places within a person's life line or ancestry to what I perceived as "knots" or "holes". My guides would proceed to bring in other agents that would disentangle knots and free the essence of the person who had come to work with me. I would then bring back what was freed with a story of its qualities and how to look after this energy or essence. When I was taken to a hole I was told by my guides to wait there for ages letting myself feel what the client felt while not taking it on for them. So I waited in the loop of time and asked a waterfall to keep cleansing me and allowing what was there with the client to be cleansed too. Eventually the guide would reappear with a story they would show me of healing to a land or people and would hand me a ball of light that would be power or an attribute that had withdrawn due to the story back in time. I would welcome the power back, waiting for it to show itself to me as a form with a message and then rattle it over the person or sing it through. Later, when Vulture Woman came to work with me, I would have her come through as a boundary setter for some of the people who came for sessions. She would know how to deeply honour the soul purpose of an individual like no other guide I had ever met and would give me important visions to bring back to them.

When I later went on to study constellation therapy and trained to be a counsellor, the Gestalt model made a lot of sense to me. I realized that when we listen to any story in the present with ears that can track back through time we are often allowing other more distant stories to be heard and healed.

The power of awareness and acknowledgment is huge. In this next simple piece of work, you will be invited to bring to awareness and acknowledge a couple of places in your own ancestry where there are holes or knots. Nature will be the healer in this.

Nature as a Healer

In Present Lifetime we looked at how putting nature and self-care first was a brilliant provider of the conditions for a connected and flowing life. Do you remember the practice with the river and the opening to your own Calling in this lifetime and then the collective Calling in this lifetime? You will remember also how initiation was seen as something that was looking to show itself and be met so that we can grow to be even more in touch with what has been previously available for us. I wonder if you can see the correlation here with the holes and knots we meet in both our own lived past and the past of our ancestral lines? These unacknowledged breaks in the initiatory cycles are looking to be brought into awareness and into the whole picture. The meaning of healing is, as you know, to bring back into the whole.

Nature is one of the greatest helpers I have found to help heal the fissures we have inherited in these times. As far as I can see, the realm of nature carries on waiting for us to consciously join it and communicate with it again.

Have a think about a part of nature that has been calling your attention a lot recently. It may be a herd of cows, a meadow or a tree or plant close by. It may be a lavender plant in your grandmother's garden. If you don't have something come to mind then you might choose to pick up a rattle and ask a member of nature to come through for you.

You need to tune in to your portal place ready for the first part of the next task, and visit the nature spot. You might also choose to connect to your portal place while at your nature spot and complete the task in one go.

EXERCISE

Nature as a Healer

Part 1—Healing the Separation

Tune in to or visit the portal place and set up space in the usual way. Feel the blanket of fern and unbroken lineage beneath your feet. Now connect with your soul and the soul guide. Feel your unbroken lineage of living with soulful interconnectedness going back through all times. Feel yourself with your connection to rose and the rose guides.

Now make a journey back to the first people again. Ask them to show you the point in human evolution where nature and humans went through something that put them out of touch with one another. There are various degrees and happenings of this throughout time. So whether you are taken to the first disconnect or a more recent episode of it, trust that you are being taken to what is most relevant and meaningful to you and your own story in this lifetime.

When you get there, allow rose and the guides to go in before you, taking compassion, healing and balm to all the places that are needing this. Feel this going to the empathic parts in you too. Then call in Vulture and know that she will go to all the places that are needing deep honouring. If you come back from this journey before you go on to Part 2, then make sure you feel rose holding everything and that you feel secure knowing that love, honouring and healing energy is prevailing.

Part 2—Healing Your Story

Visit the part of nature that has been calling you. You can take music to play or you can drum or simply be with your breath. Wear your Protector. Now merge with this member of nature as its pure essence. You can do this by asking the essence of it to be before you and then step into it or open to it filling your field. Then you simply download whatever information or energy is important for listening to whatever part in you, as a part of the whole, carries the effects of that break with nature back in time. Feel it like the deepest immersion in deep listening. Feel this listening and allowing of merging untying knots and reaching into the deepest holes within your being. You might hear the spirit of this member of nature speaking with you and bringing guidance. You might feel the ancestors also drinking deep what is their part of the story too.

After some time (say ten to twenty minutes), thank the essence of the nature being that you have merged with and then shake all around your body. Stamp your feet on the ground and return to your senses. You can also ask Vulture to sweep your aura with her feathers to bring you back to your own true clear self. Thank Vulture. You might also choose to burn some sage or spray some frankincense or myrrh to clear your aura.

How do you feel now? Take some notes.

Now you have made this first journey and know that you can travel back to any of the times of separation that are significant for you at any time. Know also that you have the places where these ancestors you have listened to as access points for wisdom and sharing information at any time. You have been drawn to them for a reason. They will be a part of your time-travelling collective.

Chapter 7

Dreaming with the Ancestors

The root of the word "ancestor" is the Latin *ante cedere,* meaning going before. If we consider the Loop of time and feel into what precedes us, then we can somehow feel into how our work with the ancestors is a lot about inheritance! We can inherit support, hope and encouragement just as we can inherit trouble, guilt and depression.

Have you ever had dreams where your ancestors have come to you with a message or a riddle? I remember after my maternal grandmother died repeatedly having dreams about the phone ringing and picking it up to find it was my grandmother trying to get through. I couldn't reach her. It took shamanic journeying a few years down the line to find out what the disconnect was and what she was trying to tell me. Conversely, I have had journeys that just won't reveal for me the answer to an ongoing health problem or worry I am asking about. I have instead put out for my dreams to reveal the answers. I remember one particular incident, when I was struck by chronic fatigue, of my dog from childhood coming through and showing me how sad I had been when she was put down. I had completely blocked my entire memories of any relationship I had had with her before she died, but it seemed that her being put down had had a profound impact on me. Once I could reconnect with her, my ability to move forward in my life with energy came back. At this station of my life something had registered that I couldn't and wouldn't go on without her any longer. I realized how much I had loved this dog!

After my cousin died, I found it so hard to accept her difficult and untimely death. After six months, she came through in a dream. She was running down a tunnel with her head on fire. I followed her. She turned round and told me that I couldn't follow her because she was further along the path than me. These words, although spoken through utterly surreal and bleak imagery, registered in me the truth that she was closer to her spiritual nature than I was and I had things to do to evolve. I saw her as she truly was and the dream transformed my way of looking at this tragic event and my life.

This week we are going to step out of ordinary time in the habitual way we do every day of our lives without fail! We are time travellers whenever we put our heads on those pillows and fall asleep. This week we enter the great portal of the unconscious and our dreams.

The Definition of Dreaming

The word "dream" is of Germanic origin, relating to the Dutch *droom*, German *Traum* and the old Saxon *drom*, meaning merriment or noise. The Old English root of dream is *drēam*, meaning joy or music. You can really see how the original meaning of dream was to do with bringing through happy sounds or emotions. Later, in the 1900s, the word became synonymous with planning or aspiring to something. It is clear from these definitions that dreaming is such a powerful part of the creation cycle!

In the mythology of some Australian Aboriginal peoples, Dreamtime, or Alcheringa, is the world that is a deeper octave of this one. Dreamtime is what is behind the manifestation of the natural world and is celebrated in ritual. Dreamtime is a place of power. I wonder if our forgetting how to work with dreaming is akin to our divide from nature and our true natures?

Opening the Doors and Inviting

Here is a practice that can help us to bring in our relationship with the dreamtime and value the time travel we have access to every single day.

EXERCISE

Creating a Dream Hoop

You are going to make yourself a dream hoop. You can find some softened willow and bend it into a circle, or perhaps you will find some twigs from a tree that you love and ask if you can weave them together. Or maybe you will take some florist's wire and weave around it some dried grasses and flowers of your choice.

While you are making the hoop, hold the intention that the hoop is a doorway of invitation through which ancestors with helpful messages or healing can enter to visit you in the night.

Activate your dream hoop by going to your portal with it and placing it in your five-stoned circle there. Open up space in the usual way. Allow the rose guides to come in and cleanse and bless your hoop's gateway. Connect with a guide for the gateway of your dream hoop and ask them some questions about dreaming. Set that the guide will be a clear, true sentinel for you and will only admit what is useful and kind.

Hang your hoop up in your bedroom or stand it on its edge on a surface close to your bed. See what happens!

Journeying into Dreams

Over the next week especially, be open to ancestors coming through to you in your dreams. Have a pad and pen by your bed to take notes immediately on waking. Not everyone remembers dreams. If this is the case for you, then don't worry. Your unconscious will have still been working. You will just have the job of seeing how the ancestors become apparent in your daytime living after the forgotten dreaming. Be aware of where your thoughts go in the day or if one of your ancestors is drawn into conversation or awareness through some other means.

Once you have felt a connection with a clear ancestor, either by dreaming or by them coming into your life in another way, then make a space to journey back into the dream space as below.

EXERCISE
Inviting In the Ancestors

Sit with a drum in front of your hoop. Connect with the portal on the land. Open space in the usual way. Feel your connection to soul and your soul guide and your Protector.

Call to mind the ancestor that has come through your dreams or that has come into your life this week. If you have a dream recorded, then journey into the dreamscape and take in the details again. If you didn't have a dream but had the experience of remembering the ancestor in another way, then feel them beyond the circle of the dream hoop.

Now hold your rose and feel the rose guides present. Connect with Future and feel her deep honouring and ability to go between life and death all of the time. Journey into the dream hoop to meet the ancestor as you gently beat your drum. Ask them why they have appeared and what you need to know from them right now. Ask them what they are looking to heal with you and what you are ready to heal with them.

Feel rose and the guides at work around you. Feel the honouring and fearlessness of Vulture. Feel how everything is in this space with your ancestor and hold the intention of healing, listening and healthy connection.

After the meeting is complete, thank your ancestor and drum yourself back through the hoop to the everyday. Close the hoop again and see the sentinel there holding it safe for you.

Write some notes.

Sometimes we have to wait a while until a dream connection happens so if you don't get the connection this time, don't worry—you can wait until later to make this journey, or simply visit an ancestor you have been waiting to go and visit for a long time.

Chapter 8

Ceremonies of Release and Surrender with the Ancestors

In the final chapter of Loop with the ancestors, we are going to work with ceremonies. Our ancestors knew well the importance of ceremony as a way of upholding connection and communication and for bringing alignment with the Earth's patterns. The ceremonies have always been a way of keeping humans and nature together and of celebrating and bringing spiritual support to rites of passage in life.

Blessing a birth, blessing a name, celebrating first steps, coming of age, first blood, womanhood, manhood, marriage, becoming a parent, children leaving home, promoting the elders, all of these are important initiation points in a life that have special guides, ancestral powers, places on the Earth

and times of the year ready to hold space for them. Part of the work with the ancestors is about tapping back into these places, helpers and times of year.

I have brought in the idea of having ceremonies of release and surrender with the ancestors to support the allowing of each of our intentions. Sometimes we can be carrying burdens and expectations for those who come before us. The weight of this and the room it takes in us can prohibit the space and conditions for what is innately our own expression and gift to come through. The work this week will be to hold a ceremony where we can hand back what isn't ours to the ancestors and also see it being listened to and held for our ancestors too.

I expect as you are reading this something might already be coming to mind!

Meaning of Ceremony

The root of "ceremony" in Middle English is *cerymonye,* from the Latin *caerimonia* or *caeremonia*, or later *cerimonia*. It means sacredness, reverence, a sacred rite.

I often explain ceremony as simply being something that states, "this is *really, really* important!" Having importance placed on certain things means they can become a priority and the energy can flow to them. Honouring can happen!

Our lives are a series of rituals that when repeated set a pattern of existence. Rituals are kind of mini ceremonies without the grand audience, but they set a tone too. If we place importance on going to the shops and watching TV then these become our ceremonies and we are tied into consumerism and what the media promote for us. However, if we go to the shops and watch TV with the intention of buying food for a special celebratory meal and with the intention of watching a film with a storyline that is inspiring or particular to our lives right now, then we can create more empowered flow for ourselves and our lives. If we fill our lives with walks to sacred sites and special nature places then you can see also that we are opening to bring meaning to the places on the Earth and to get to know nature in a deeper way. Everything we do is an opportunity for choosing meaningful or disempowered living. This is not to say we can't relax and go with the flow and see what comes our way when we shop or watch TV. It is just to point out the importance of building meaning for ourselves and not having it imposed on us.

A ceremony is a special event that calls in the audience of that which transcends the present moment and invites all physical and non-physical realm eyes to attend to it. You have been working with a ceremony every time you open space in your portal place to visit the ancestors and every time you invite your ancestors to come through in dreams. However, some ceremonies are bigger than others. We anticipate them, look forward to them and set them up with an exceptional reverence. Let this ceremony be one such ceremony.

The Burden of Unfinished Business

I talked earlier about Gestalt therapy and the idea of something needing to show itself appearing in our lives for listening to and allowing previous incomplete initiations to be brought to a close. Another expression for this kind of incompleteness is "unfinished business".

EXERCISE
Preparation for Ceremony

The ceremony of release and surrender will be for your life and also for your ancestors in their resonant stories.

To prepare for the ceremony I invite you to do the following:

1 Select a special costume or clothing to wear so you can be "Release of the Old and Fresh New Start".

2 On separate cards, write down the things that you notice still have a hold in your life and draw your attention back.

3 Select more cards to be the unfinished business of the ancestors. Feel into the ancestral lines and locate areas where there is a weight or heaviness. Work intuitively with how many you select. You don't need to know what it is, just feel the weight of something.

4 Select an evening or day for this ceremony and anticipate it. Make a journey in advance to visit all of the ancestors and the guides you are working with in Loop. Ask them to prepare with you and if they have any special guidance for you on what to include or do.

The Time Machine of Reuniting

EXERCISE

Ceremony of Release and Surrender

Go to your portal place or connect. Wear your costume. Take with you the cards, drum and rattle.

Set up space. Feel Fern and the carpet of fern travelling through an unbroken lineage. Feel the unbroken lineage of your soul through time. Call in Rose and the guides. Call in Vulture and the power of deep honouring.

Acknowledge your ability to travel in the great loop of time and feel yourself connecting to the engine of it all.

Call everything in to bear witness.

Speak your intention to release and surrender for both yourself and the ancestors whose cards you have brought.

Simply drum. Let every drumbeat call release and surrender. Call on the beings that understand release and surrender. Direct your drumbeats to the vibrations of energy written on the cards from your own life and to the weight you felt that called you to choose cards for the ancestors. Feel Rose also going to those places with compassion and deep listening. Feel Fern bearing witness at points in history.

When you finally feel complete, thank everything. Rejoice!

Close the ceremony. Release yourself and everything. Tear up the cards to be recycled later. Know the work is done to release what they previously held. Scatter rose petals.

Write what comes to mind now for the new space.

With our time in Ancestors complete, find a way to give thanks for their lives, their initiations and their truth. Let them know you are always willing to hear their messages. Then come firmly back into the present moment.

Sit down and take in what is around you and how it feels to have immersed yourself in this scene of travelling into the realm of the ancestors.

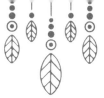

Scene 4: Future Pathways

In this scene we are going to be having fun connecting with the future ones! Lotus, orca, python and the waters of the Earth join us in an adventure of cleansing and creating a positive vision.

Introduction to Future Pathways

Something that has made me much happier in life is connecting with the future ones. The future ones to me live in a land of brightness and a frequency of positive energy. They are also very grounded on their planet. I love them so much. They are the ones who, like mothers or fathers who hold out arms to a newly walking child, cheer me on. When I speak to the future generations I don't feel them as separate to the gods and goddesses and animal archetypes, I feel them as an embodiment of them. It is to these people that I constantly look and they help me to regain my faith in humanity. I think perhaps most of my ideas come from them! I think this is what is said of all the visionaries, isn't it, that they have ideas before their time?

Accepting that we have a future has been for me the most positive way to accept and be responsible for my time in the present. I honestly feel that many of the best ideas have yet to happen. Enlightenment comes from the possibility of what can be. I think the striving of humans to keep on developing is made from this.

The element for Future Pathways is water. Here is an exercise connecting with water to help us to prepare. You will need to fill a small bowl or dish of water before you begin.

EXERCISE

Connecting with Water Element

Come firmly into the place of present. Place the bowl of water on a surface where you can be aware of it. Set the intention that you will be opening to the element of water a lot in your time with future. Feel the water as having the ability to absorb, take on impressions, wash, open and allow travel. Feel the water able to communicate with the water in you too. As you know, the human body consists of around sixty per cent water. Feel water as an element and a spirit both in front of you in the bowl and then within your body. Maybe have a look into the surface of the water with this openness to the quality and living energy of water in mind. What do you feel like when you connect with water as a spirit and as a living energy? How does it feel to think of yourself as being made of so much water and for the spirit of water to flow through you? What is water communicating to you as you contemplate it as a medium?

Settle with your thoughts of water and notice how you are feeling and how this might change your view of yourself. You are going to look around you now and bring your watery knowing more into the present moment. Find your everyday senses working and engaging with your surroundings. Sight, hearing, smell, touch, taste, how are these senses in you? Be aware of your power to sense and feel a relationship with everything that is with you in the now. Then bring your attention to the way you are feeling this moment. Where is your mind going? What is on your mind? What is well and truly lodged and Looped in your mind? Be allowing and with all of it. All of this information will simply show you how you are with your present lived story.

Come back to your relationship with water again, both in the bowl in front of you and in your body. How does your sense of yourself and this moment change when you do this?

So now, with water in the front of your consciousness, have a think about your life. Do you like it? Do you feel fulfilled? What do you like about it? What is challenging or brings sadness or worry in your life? If you were to project yourself into the future, what do you think you would like to focus on in order to make something change for you? Bring your thoughts to the things that you are working to accept as much as to the things you might be hoping to bring into being. Think about your life dreams. Are there any you can think of that are especially important to you? Bring water in, keep your relationship with water and the way it works central to this exercise. There might even be some clearing or soothing that happens with water being so present for you. Write some notes.

Here you are in the present, aware of water and mapping your time present with time future. In this present state of physical presence, with water at the forefront of everything, bring in the concept of "ideas". You don't need to do anything except be open to them. Hold this space for a couple of minutes and see what happens. What happens in the present moment? Where do ideas seem to come from?

One of the things we will be looking to do in Future Pathways is to make sure that we can draw our energy to be available for us in the present, while having a clear vision and trajectory into what my guide calls "the future life map line". We will be playing with this field of "ideas". So let this just settle as an experience now and simply permit your awareness of the bowl of water to become more focused. In your mind's eye, ask the bowl of water to support you with developing clear vision in the moment.

Over the next period of time when you work with the future ones, keep the bowl of water topped up and in your space. Water has long been an element for divination through different traditions.

We are ready! Welcome to the watery doors of the future! Come in and let's meet the important supporters for this territory.

Chapter 9

Waters of the Earth

In Future Pathways, we are in the zone of water as an element. The spirit animal for this direction is orca and the plant spirit is lotus.

Let's jump into the ocean of time and find out what orca and lotus have to show us.

Orca

Orca (*Orcinus orca*) is also known as killer whale. It is a toothed whale and is the largest member of the oceanic dolphin family. Orcas, which have a diverse diet, can be found in each of the world's oceans. Many indigenous cultures value them highly. There are some indigenous American clans who have orca as their crest. They feature in many mythologies around the world. The film *Whale Rider* is about the Maori relationship with this sacred being. To the Kwakiutl tribe of New Zealand, killer whales share souls with humans in a cycle of connected life forms.

Orca has an amazing capacity to sense and to hold majesty and focus. It can survive the harshest of climates. Orca has a great power in holding its own, while fostering community, camaraderie, loyalty and longevity. You can feel the stability and the dependability of the orca as an ally. Orca calls us to be leaders and guides while working to be a part of a team. The importance of family and pods is emphasized. They mate for life. Their association with water and their appearance on the surface alludes to their ability to reveal hidden knowledge. What a great creature to be working with to help us in our communication with the future ones!

EXERCISE
Journeying with Orca

Sit in front of your bowl of water, or go out to visit a water site. Make the intention to make a journey to visit orca. When you connect with orca, ask the beautiful creature to show you how it works and introduce you to their family. Be curious about what orca feels about the future. See if you can find any information from orca about the folklore which says humans and orca souls have alternating life incarnations. Ask if you may merge with her/him. How does it feel to be orca? Is it familiar? When it is time to come back (after fifteen to twenty minutes) fully detach from the mammal and thank them. Leave a natural offering in the ocean or scatter to the winds.

Lotus

In Buddhist lore, the lotus flower signifies purity, spirituality and self-cleansing. In Hinduism, lotus represents themes such as fertility, prosperity, spirituality and eternity. The natural phenomenon of a pure lotus rising from within murky waters and sustaining its beauty is synonymous with the path of transformation and the process of clearing. Lotus has come to be felt as a symbol of peace.

Layne Redmond writes about the importance of the lotus goddess with the frame drum. The chakra energy points in the human body are in yogic theory each spinning with a different vibration, and connect to bring spirit into matter (crown to base chakra) and then back again. A lotus represents each chakra with an ever-increasing number of petals from root chakra (four) to crown chakra (thousands). You can imagine how this symbolism honours the lotus as an inspirer in the health system of the human and the process of realization and enlightenment. We will look at this more closely in one of the later sections!

EXERCISE

Merging with Lotus

For now, let's open up our relationship with lotus by picking up our drums and saying hello to the lotus in nature. Visit the lotus in a journey and ask to merge with it. What does it feel like to be lotus? Perhaps you can visit the different loti within your chakras too while merging with lotus, to see what effect this brings. You could perhaps see if you can make some sounds with each chakra in turn to express the frequency of the chakra lotus you are visiting. Root, sacral, solar plexus, heart, throat, third eye and crown are the places of the chakras as they work up the body. Connect with the sound of the drum and the lotus goddess as you do this as well. After about fifteen minutes come back and thank lotus for letting you merge and have this experience. Have a big drink of water. How do you feel about lotus now?

Precious Time

Recently I have really been feeling the importance of feeling time as precious. I came off social media for a while to bring my focus much more into the now and also to bring more time to producing material that could go into books. I have since had to go back onto social media as part of an agreement with an agent, but I know that I have a much different relationship with it because I have more understanding of the value of time. Another thing I have been working on is helping myself, when I am indoors writing or painting, to keep connected to nature. In order to do this, I have been purposefully seeing myself as a nature being. In my personal study, it seems that the more I feel myself as a part of the flow of nature serving something that is natural and clear, the more easily I can live in tune with myself. Time can be more precious for me.

EXERCISE

Honouring the Precious

Make a list of what is precious to you in life and have the list in a space where you can read it every day. This can help to bring attention to what is true for you and help you to value this more.

Time as a Woven

Most spiritual traditions have deities who are in charge of time. The way that humans experience the happenings of time is often called fate. Fate is felt as an almost supernatural power that has a way of moving through our lives. In Roman and Greek mythology, there were three goddesses referred to who presided over the birth and life of humans. They were called Clotho, Lachesis and Atropos and were collectively known as the three Fates. People's destiny was thought of as a thread spun, measured and cut by them.

In Slavic mythology, the fairies are linked with fate. Some of the other deities associated with this idea of destiny being somehow in the hands of something bigger are the Norns (Germanic); Dalia (Baltic); the Anunnaki (Mesopotamia); and Ori (Yoruba).

Weaving

When my children were young, I was fortunate to live close to the sea and to places where seals hung out. I used to make sure we went to the beach two or three times a week. One day, I read that seals liked being sung to and could be charmed to come closer by a special seal song. So I went about divining a song for the seals and singing it for them. It worked! I was able to attract seals with this song pretty much wherever I went that seals resided. In fact on a couple of occasions, a seal popped up right next to me when I was swimming in the sea. I know the seals as part of the weaving tapestry of life.

Songs are amazing as a way of opening connection. Many people who work with the dying sing as a way of opening the realms and bringing peace to the one who is about to cross. I sang the whole way through the final night of my friend Cathy's life before she died. I stayed up, making up songs with a buzzard wing that was her spirit animal.

We are going to help open the veils with our song and sing to the future ones!

Future Time Travel

⬩

EXERCISE

Setting Up Future Time Travel

It is time to visit your portal place again. Set yourself up in the usual way, either on site or remotely. Feel the fern going back through time like a carpet. For time travel to the future, you are going to feel in front of you a river of light. This light will be similar to water and you will be able to travel with orca as if through water, but it will be more than water too!

As you stand ready to journey, feel your feet firmly planted in the present time and feel those chakras, each with a lotus. Ask to connect to orca again with the intention of visiting the future ones. You aren't going to go into a place of prophecy or prediction; we are working from a place of knowing that power comes in each moment. Just as we have the power to change our focus and do the work to raise our vibration and connect with something more supportive in each moment, the future has this power too. However, we are working with the idea that the future can be better for everyone because of what we choose to connect with and include right now. What this will be and how it will come about is not for our knowing in this work.

When you have a clear connection with orca and the river of light, set the intention clearly that you are only going to connect with what is powerful and true in the future. Feel through the river for the future ones who will be standing there in their clear, bright and healed version.

With orca, you are now going to create a song linking to them. You can drum or rattle too. But create a tune that will become your signature tune for calling to the power and wisdom of the future ones. Try recording it on a device so you don't forget it.

Chapter 10

A Cleaning-Up Job

It's time to do a bit of cleaning now! As we work with the future ones, we are very much working with the present time too. Whenever I hold a party I always have to clean and tidy the house in preparation for people's arrival. If I don't do this, my channels are just not properly open and relaxed to receive them. Often when I have a big piece of work, tidying up suddenly seems like the most important thing to do. When I was a teenager, my mum would laugh and call me a procrastinator. I would laugh too because it is partly true. But there is something else there about clearing channels in preparation for an arrival. A ritual of cleaning and washing the self precedes all great ceremonies. In preparation for receiving the future ones, let's prepare to invest some of our minutes in a clearing preparation.

The Dumping Ground of the Future

When you think about your past are you aware of having any negative thoughts and helpless feelings about your future? Can you recall any moments of thinking something like, "Oh I could never do that so I won't even try"? We can unconsciously dump a lot of fatalism onto our future lives by the thoughts we have about ourselves. How about the media? Do you sometimes find you have to stop watching news or reading about events because the negativity gets you down? Even if I am positive about my life and my future, I can be quickly knocked down by the weight of negativity about the future of the planet and the current state of affairs.

I wonder what our lives would be today if we had had a whole caring and encouraging set of people in past history? I wonder what we would live inside if the previous generations had been led by visionaries who listened to everyone, and kept the traditions of listening to the whole of nature and communing with spirits? I wonder what would have been our today if there had been people in the past looking to the future and thinking carefully about what would help? I know that many, many did and I am so grateful for them. But history books show us just how much the Earth and all of its beings and spirits were disenfranchized and not respected through time. For a lot of our ancestral governing systems, the future stopped being something sacred to look after. Life somehow became about survival, competition and being secure.

I think it is clear that the dumping that has been made on this ground is the dumping of responsibility of care, blindness for awareness of the future ones and a passing on of a responsibility to sort things out in the moment. It has also been the dumping of a schema that doesn't hold respect for the many ways, an inclusion of multiple dimensions and seeing nature as *animus* too.

The Power of Visualization

One of the adages I use most in my work is probably the one that goes "energy flows where attention goes". What we focus on can become manifest!

When I am ready for a move, I always paint a picture of a house I am aiming for next. When I painted and then found my last house, it had everything I had hoped for. However, it also had a sauna. I hadn't included that in my grand design. I found myself going, "You can't have a sauna, Carol." I had imagined I couldn't be the type of woman who would have a sauna in her home. I caught myself limiting what I could receive. So I stopped myself and applied to rent it. I got the lease. The house had a balcony too (also in my painting). The balcony overlooked the River Tay and the hills behind Dundee. I spent the next two months (that led on to eight years) being presented with the most amazing views through huge bay windows and found myself constantly hearing myself thinking the words, "I am so lucky. I am so lucky." Well guess what, my life got a lot easier from then on. I know that it was the self-talk I was constantly hearing come automatically from my brain. Visualization is both visual and mental in words and attitudes. It is powerful stuff.

Recapitulation

Years ago, at a time when I was really run-down, I was introduced to the practice of recapitulation by one of my Toltec teachers who was then known as Raven Smith. Recapitulation is a real cleaning-up exercise, scrying through the memories of the mind and returning to scenes to play them back like a film. You next walk through these scenes with a guide and, keeping a detached point of view, breathe out what you have taken on from an environment or situation and then breathe in what you have given away. I usually have my guide holding a protective cocoon around me and ask that everything that is breathed out is transmuted to light. Transmutation is a practice that Sandra Ingerman introduced me to in her Medicine for the Earth work.

I spent nine months in my early forties going into pockets of my life retrieving power and clearing my energy field. It was wonderful!

Lotus Cleansing

EXERCISE

Lotus Cleansing for Yourself

Here is a cleansing exercise working with lotus in which we will work to clear already projected negative thoughts onto yourself from the past!

First have a few minutes to reflect back into the timeline of your life. You can write a list or draw a diagram too if it helps. Remember some time when you were particularly low or felt a lot of helplessness or shame about yourself. It can also be a time when you had a projection of not very kind thoughts on to you by someone else. You don't want to engage with the feelings that were there, so make sure you are able to be reasonably detached when you are making some notes.

Pick one of the times that isn't too emotive for you to work with. You will find, as you work through, that you will have more energy to be a practitioner for yourself with things on a list like this.

Now start playing some relaxing music or a drumming track. Connect with lotus and feel the lotus of each of your chakras. Take some deep breaths. Now connect with your body Protector, rose, so that you can feel strength and extra support there for you.

As you connect with lotus and the lotus in each of your chakras, start to hum. Feel yourself like a lotus cleaner. Perhaps you have a feather duster. Travel through this time humming with lotus as you voyage. Let the thoughts you were having then be blessed with the energy of release and purity. Let your humming be this pure, strengthening and opening energy too.

When you feel complete (after fifteen to twenty minutes probably), give thanks to lotus and rose. Come back to the present and stamp your feet on the ground. Open a window and get some air. The first cleaning-up job for your life has happened!

EXERCISE

Lotus Cleansing for the Collective

For this next task find another day when you are feeling quite strong in yourself. This time you are going to journey out into the collective to times of critical mass for the results of the negative thoughts. This could be today or it could be a time in the more distant future.

So, feel yourself again with rose and lotus. Stand at the place of the portal or connect with it remotely. You can use a drum or rattle to assist you on this journey if you like. Feel the river of light and orca with you. Feel the power of lotus as itself and within your chakra points. Remember to hum!

Now, simply working with orca and lotus together, let orca guide you to a place on the planet either now or in the future when there are a lot of negative thoughts or feelings of futility. Be sure to keep your Protector rose with you and all about you, so you don't have to feel all of this. Simply allow lotus to go into this place with its purity and its ability to release and bring peace. Listen to orca and feel the guidance orca gives you as she/he supports this operation. Feel the guides that work with lotus transmuting and bringing strength and compassion to the places where it is needed.

After ten to fifteen minutes, bring yourself back. Feel the river of light and orca and then thank everything and say goodbye, before closing the connection you have to the portal in the usual way and coming back to this time and place. Remember every little helps and you don't have to take anything on. Visualize that lots of people today can join you in this too!

Write some notes!

Chapter 11

Journeying and the Oracle

Let's open a little bit of study now with some of my good friends from the distant past. These souls are famous for reading and gently scouring the realms of the future ones. They are expert designers of the architecture for the creation of positive flow. Let's go on a visit to the Oracle at Delphi in Ancient Greece. Let's meet the priestesses of the Pythia.

Python and the Mythical

In Greek mythology, python was the serpent (represented as a medieval-style dragon) who lived at the centre of the Earth. The ancient Greeks believed python's home to be at Delphi and its powers were felt through the spring water that ran underneath this place and the steam of which filled the temple room, inducing trance.

There are lots of stories about the python and I won't go into them here, but what I will tell is the story of the priestesses who gathered at this place of the python. They were known as the Pythia and individually they took the role of being the Oracle for Ancient Greek times. The Oracle divined information about the future. Influential leaders would travel miles to consult the Oracle over important matters. The Oracle would work with python to go into a trance and to bring the visions for the age through to the people.

The serpent resided in myth along with the other gods and goddesses of the Greek Parthenon. The relationship that these people had with the different members of nature and the mythical ones that they connected with in the tapestry of their lives helped them to collectively live in flow with a deeper level of knowing. They were always weaving with the power of nature and its part in the whole show with the play of humans.

The truth is that nature has never left the mythical! It stands in the everyday and the mythical all of the time. I think it is maybe just waiting for you and me to join it there! When we choose to communicate with the life forms around us and appreciate that everything has a clear soul,

174

just like us, then we begin to understand how we can possibly be a part of the greater mythology too. The goddesses and gods were each deities for expressions of life and their connection to the animals and nature was a widely accepted knowing. It is obvious that some had roles of being closer to the centre of life than others. Just like we worked with the fern as an ancient plant spirit and found a way to travel back in time with its unbroken lineage, we can work with the serpent too. When I have journeyed into this, the dragon serpents have always come through as being one of the first creator spirits. They are also, in their reptilian way, possibly the first land creatures to come out of the water. Imagine how deeply connected to the mysteries of creation they are.

EXERCISE

Journeying to Python

Here is a simple journey to make to python. Put on a drumming track. Journey to connect with lotus and orca. Ask to be taken to Delphi to meet python and the priestesses there. See what you can find out!

Nature and the Mythical

EXERCISE

Connecting to the Mythical through Nature

Visit your portal or work remotely with it. Set up space in the usual way. Connect with fern and see the carpet going right back through time. Imagine somewhere on that timeline the time of the Oracle at Delphi. Recall how nature holds the mythical all of the time and feel the vibration in the lines of when and where this was understood. Remember this way of consciously feeling and revering life still exists in many cultures on the planet today.

Feel the river of light and orca in front of you. Sing the song to the future ones. Feel them there. Ask to sing both to the humans and to the nature beings. Feel them all. Ask to be singing to the mythical. How are the mythical, the people and the whole of nature in those times? As you sing, feel that sense of connection and belonging with the mythical and nature flowing with you too in this time.

After a while, say thank you and bring yourself back to this time. Say goodbye to orca and detach from the past and future and close the portal and your opening to it with the method you have learnt. Write some notes.

Oracle Anew

EXERCISE

Setting Up Your Oracle Space

At your portal you are going to set up your very own Oracle place! Please do this journey remotely.

Set up space for a journey going to explore this. You can rattle or play a drumming track. Make your journey feeling the past and fern behind you and the river of light in front of you. Merge with lotus and ask that you connect with the mythical aspect of you through lotus. Perhaps you will feel yourself become a lotus goddess or god or some other deity that is related to your abilities in this lifetime.

Ask to find the members who will hold this Oracle space for you. You will be connecting with the serpent in the Earth next week.

Now visualize a place for the children who are coming through on the planet at the moment. Feel the human children, orca children and all species of beings and plant and tree worlds as children. Feel your mythical self with lotus and the ones who hold this Oracle space with you going into the river of light with orca. Feel light blessings being drawn from this river and being taken to and shone onto the children.

Feel them blessing you too! The Children are leading us!

Come back to the present moment. Thank everything. Disconnect and close the portal connection. How do you feel now? Take some notes.

Chapter 12

Unity

The Healing of Prejudice

If healing is about restoring wholeness and allowing everything to have its place, then it is quite clear that division and prejudice is one of the leading factors behind the world not being able to come together and unite. In this final chapter of our journey with Loop, our work will be to bring to the fore these places of prejudice and see if something can be restored.

Unity Chant

Have you ever been in a choir or at a concert or somewhere where everyone is singing along in unison and noticed the power of this? It's like a wave of immense strength isn't it? I know someone who goes to football matches just for the power of being in the crowd and feeling the togetherness with a cause and the power of the collective singing!

Vibration, as we looked at with the chakras and lotus, is the seed of creation. In the task below we will be singing our song to the future ones, honouring their power, connection and love. Then we will be inviting the future ones to join us in song and to direct the song to places of prejudice in the lines of our current life and beyond.

🍃

EXERCISE
Unity Chant

You can work remotely for this task. Try playing some choral music as a background. Open the portal in the usual way, feeling fern behind you with its carpet. Connect with the river of light and orca. Merge with lotus and feel your chakra lotus in each chakra spinning. Connect with your mythical self again. Sing your song to the future ones.

As you feel them come into place in front of you, far in the future, notice the landscape and all of its nature beings and sing to them too. See how the mythical and the everyday stand together. Feel orca swimming to and fro through time and the interchange between human and orca lifetimes.

When you feel the vibration of song from the future ones too, settle your voice and see if you can divine a song or tune from them to you that is a song that can be the power of the new, from a place beyond prejudice.

Sing the song or make the notes with them.

Now, with orca flowing through the river of light, with you standing in your place in the present and future ones in their place, see orca weaving the power of this song and taking its strength and energy of wholeness and unity to the places where it is needed. Pick up your rattle and rattle when you feel it getting to these places. Let the power of the unity song be taken to places of prejudice both today and through the future lines.

After about fifteen minutes or more, let your voice become quiet and thank the future ones. Know that this work can continue outside of time and space.

Close the connection to the portal in the usual way. Say goodbye to orca for now and come back. How do you feel?

Cord Making

There is a scientific theory that DNA is the common thread that links every living thing with a single primeval ancestor. The DNA that runs through us runs through everything. It links us with a web of interconnectedness.

In spiritual circles there is much speculation about whether we have more strands in our human DNA than the two we are currently believed to have. It's a bit like the unused parts of our brain theory. So keep an open mind and go with your own guidance in the next task!

✑

EXERCISE

Cord Making

Set up space in the usual way to go on a journey with your portal to the future ones. Connect to orca and lotus and open up to the river of light. Ask the future ones to show you the full potential of your DNA from their perspective. Ask them to show you its threads and the colour and power of its threads. Come back after thanking everyone and make a picture with coloured pencils of what you were shown.

Making the Sacred Python

✑

EXERCISE

Creating a DNA Python

In this task we are going to continue with the idea that energy flows where attention goes and that what we do today has an effect and a vibration on everything that happens in the future. We are going to make a sacred DNA python out of threads. Source threads that are akin to the DNA colours you were shown.

Play some music that is similar to the energy of the journey you made. Connect with the future ones again and merge with the vibration of what you were shown in the journey when you asked the question.

As you connect and as the music is playing, take the threads of the colours you were shown. Tie the threads together and then plait them to be a cord that can be the sacred python of life in its most energized and full potential self. Tie the threads together again when you are complete.

Come out of the journey and give thanks to everything. Wear the cord as a bracelet, anklet or necklace so that you can be reminded of this vibration wherever you go.

Serpent Lines

As you will remember from the Visionary Quest section in Calling, the Earth has an energy network in its make-up, just like the human body has with its chakra points and meridians. These are known as leys in Britain and as song lines in the Australian Aboriginal traditions. Special pathways like the Camino del Norte in northern Spain are valued as healing pathways too. These pathways are also known as dragon or serpent lines.

Originally where these lines crossed were temple sites for time travel and for connecting with the other worlds. You may know the classic Outlander books and TV series, where a portal is a standing circle in Scotland. I love to divine these lines with divining rods and follow them. You often find that the altars of churches are positioned on the crossing point of these lines. I went for a walk yesterday afternoon and noticed that two of the churches in our village (our village with its small population has five churches) were built right next to one another, with another one straight across the road! As I tuned in I was aware of beautiful energy.

EXERCISE

Feeling the Serpent Power

For the final journey in Future pathways, open the portal in the usual way. Connect with the energy of your DNA in its true potential. Connect with the fern carpet of the past and then open the river of light to connect with the future ones. I wonder whom these future ones are who have come through for you? You must have such an important place with these people. Take some time to honour and thank them.

Ask the future ones to connect with the clear vibration of the Earth in those times and to show you the serpent energy as it exists in the land. When you have a clear feeling of it, connect back in time to the python who existed in the land of the Temple of the Oracle. Now open to feeling the serpent energy in the land. Simply stand or sit there with the future ones, the Pythia priestesses and your own true knowing, observing the serpent power of the land and the waters. Feel the past honouring and the future honouring of this flowing as a continuum into the land of modern times and the serpent power on the planet. What does this feel like? Be aware of the portal you have set up and feel the connection to the serpent power beneath your feet.

After a few minutes, thank everyone, say goodbye in turn and come back to the present moment. Disconnect from and close the portal with your usual sign and method.

Simply set the intention that you will feel the power of the land and its energy lines and see that each place can have its function and ways too for the days you live on Earth.

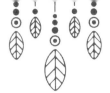

Scene 5: Wishes for the Future

Reflecting on Future Pathways

It is time to reflect back now on your experience in Future Pathways and to make some wishes for the future.

Have a look back at the intention you set for this project. How is it looking? What has opened in you? What have you discovered? How has connecting with the future ones changed you?

Open a circle for yourself in the usual way and call in the orca souls. Write a letter to your future self from where you are now. Let yourself share whatever feels really important to be known. Now ask the orca if they would like to write a letter through you. With permission, write a letter on behalf of orca to the future orca and humans. Write a letter to the whole of nature in the future, knowing what you do about your place in nature today.

When you have finished, read what you have written.

Then feel yourself taking a position in the future. Write back to you as "the future" sharing whatever feels really important to be known.

Put the letter in a special place to be read at an important stage in your later life.

Finale

Vision Hoop

So here we are at the finale of *Shamanic Dreaming*. We are coming to the close of our play of life in two Acts. As with all good finales, we will be wrapping up some of the themes of this play. In Finale, there is the creation of a ceremony that may take the vibrancy of the experiences through these pages into our lives to come.

We are going to make a Vision Hoop!

I remember many moons ago I made a trip to Rishikesh in India to study yoga. In the ashram where I was staying, there was a framed picture on the wall of one of the rooms. On it were the words: "Life without a plan is like a house without a blueprint." For some reason, this quote stayed with me and what is more, it completely captured my imagination. I started to wonder about the grand design for life. I thought if I could tap into it somehow in an architect's way, then maybe I would be able to help affect the future for the better. I became a bit obsessed with the idea of a blueprint and started to excavate for it through meditations and artwork. I really think this quote planted a seed for the Visionary ideas that have flowed through me in the years since.

In our finale, we are going to be architects working with this blueprint. We are going to make a hoop out of vision. Maybe you have worked out that the blueprint, of course, is vision!

How is your relationship with vision doing at the end of this play in life? Is it calling in the same way as when we began? Are you feeling it calling through a multiplicity of lenses now? In this finale piece of the making of the Vision Hoop, we will call in the hoop bearers as we have got to know them through Calling and Loop.

The natural place for the creation of our Vision Hoops will be at our very own headquarters for this book—in the triangle of presence, nature, knowing and trust at the place of each of our special trees!

Give yourself time to have a bit of a dress rehearsal first. Have a read through the finale below and collect together what you might need before you step into the completing scene at your tree. I am really holding the thought that the making of the Vision Hoop can be a dynamic act of power and creativity for everything that has been awoken in you over the course of working with this book. I am seeing it setting the way for you in this great theatre of life and all that is beyond. I am seeing it clearly wielding a healing and joyful vision that is both your own and that of the planet in these times.

Vision Hoop Ceremony

On a day that feels right for you (maybe a new moon, full moon or special day to you), take yourself to your tree, carrying the hoop for dreaming you made in Act 2 Scene 3: Ancestral Pathways. You might choose to take a drum or tambourine with you too so you can gently make a beat. Or perhaps you will work with the simple sounds of nature holding space.

Carrying your hoop for dreaming, circle the tree a number of times, asking it if it is happy to be your space holder for the Vision Hoop ceremony. I am imagining it will feel right, but if it doesn't it will be likely that you will be guided to work with another tree on the land that you will be guided to.

Visualize a grove of trees around the space. See this as a place of resources, taking out what isn't needed and bringing in what is called for and can listen best. Set a strong intention right now that the only purpose of this ceremony is to honour the Vision Hoop and to set a strong positive intention for the life of all. Only that which is in support of this is invited.

Guides of the land that come in now guide everything else and they will take them to places on the Earth's surface set up for healing. This will happen without your needing to know about it.

Now sit or stand with the tree. Perhaps you will have taken a fold-up chair with you. Feel yourself sitting on the trajectory of the circle you have just walked. Know that you are sitting with the compass that holds the elements for you and the bearings of North, South, East and West. Be curious about where you are seated or standing geographically. Are you in the east or the northwest, for example? Trust your instincts or the conditions that arose to put you on this spot. Gently drum or acknowledge the four directions and their elements as you start to invite in the wide circle of participants who have helped to prepare the energy for this hoop with you through your time in this play.

Ask the tree in the centre to hold all the dimensions and times for you and feel it reaching high into the sky and then deep into the ground. Imagine the roots as the past and the branches as the future and imagine a Loop of light moving round to join the past with the future. Ask this Loop to come and meet the outer edges of the horizontal circle you are standing in so that you can feel yourself inside an energetic orb that includes all times and frequencies and everything that is made of the elements in physicality and everything that can exist in the realms of spirit.

Drumming or tapping gently on your tambourine, or simply allowing the sounds of nature to hold the rhythm for you, call in your Protector, the Nature guide and Pathfinder guides and feel them holding space for you. Thank the ones we have met in turn, as you invite them in to join the circle:

- your intention for Calling and Loop
- yourself right now in the present
- your three brains and its two hemispheres
- the ten or eleven dimensions
- nature and all of the beings of nature

In particular:
- the weather spirits
- the birds
- the trees
- the fae

- the animals
- the animal archetypes and their associated deities
- the fire of your passion and intention
- all the humans in present times
- all who live in this plane in present times
- land
- hedgehog
- rose
- the human ancestors
- all who lived on this plane in past times as ancestors
- sky
- vulture
- fern
- the waters of the Earth
- the human future ones
- all who live on this plane in future times
- orca
- lotus
- the dreamtime
- all others who would like to be included

Just give yourself the time to feel the circle growing. Come more and more into the present moment. Connect in with knowing, nature and trust and feel yourself as a part of nature and this incredible community of listening, caring, wanting to be included, valuable beings that we are part of. Acknowledge it as an orchestra through all times and dimensions. Open your senses to the symphony that is always there.

Try saying this word: "harmony".

Hold the sentiment of harmony in your heart as you put down your drum and pick up the physical hoop. Look through your hoop to the future above, the past below and through all the dimensions. Look through the hoop to all of the four directions in turn and to everything that is on this planet right now. Look through the hoop and feel the vision of harmony moving from your heart and through the eyes and the hands as you hold it. Be open too to the vision of harmony coming from the other side of the hoop to you.

Do this for a number of minutes. You might like to sing the song the future ones gave you, or just allow a new tune that is harmony to move through you. Perhaps you need to move and dance. Whatever feels most harmonious or apt, do it!

Next, hold the hoop and say the word "love". Feel love moving out from you and coming to reach you from beyond. As you do this, ask for the power to hold the vision and to wield this power to be with you and all beings for the good of all.

And finally, ask to connect with Vision that calls through you and everything through all times, places, frequencies and possibilities. Ask Vision to come through as the one with the power to create the blueprint with you and all beings. You might want to put down the hoop and thank it for all that it represents for you and all of us to be able to drum or tap your tambourine so that you can fully and energetically connect with Vision. Ask Vision to come into a colour, a shape and then a form for you. Dance with Vision. Get to know Vision even better. Ask that Vision stays close to you and that you get to know even more the other ones who are working dedicatedly with vision and harmony in these times.

Thank everyone and everything that has worked with you in this play. Then, as with all good finales, take a bow with them all. A bow is one of the most trusting and honouring acts we can do. When we bow we say, "I am not afraid and I trust and honour you. I am not above you. I am willing to be vulnerable and humble to you. I have faith in you." When we bow together we feel that sentiment from one another too. We become as one.

Feel the curtains close now and notice how the members of this community we have connected with through *Shamanic Dreaming: A Play In Two Acts,* scatter out through the wings, back to their stations in space and time.

Take some breaths. Feel your Protector with you, helping you to ground and come fully into your everyday life. Release yourself officially from this play.

As you pick up the hoop, coming more and more back into your everyday life, and you take the first steps to walk back to your home, I wonder, as the scenes behind this one dissolve in your mind to permit you to take refuge in this clear realm you know as home again, if you can see the faint outlines of a buffalo woman smiling at you?

I see you smile back.

Overview of Exercises

Act 1: Calling

The Way of Conversation	46
Plotting the Quest Spaces	48
Setting Up Your Tree Headquarters	49
Weather Calling	60
Weather Responding	60
Bird Calling	63
Bird Responding	64
Tree Meeting	66
Tree Understanding	67
Fae Meeting	71
Fae Opening to Vision	71
Brain Attunement	79
Animal Dream	82
Drumming	84
Archetypal Landscape Meeting	91

Act 2: Loop

Nature (with Presence)	103
Nature (with Presence of Others)	104
Being Knowing	107
Being Trust	108
Connecting with Hedgehog	114
Connecting with Kairos and Chronos	116
Exploring Ego and Shapeshifter	118
Opening Up Space and Senses and Setting the Dial	121
Rose Soul Protector	123
Working with the Water Cycles	128

Connecting to the Greater Force of Water	129
Engaging with the Mysteries of Creation	133
Opening the Portal	134
Connecting to the Sky Element	142
Visiting Vulture	143
Attuning to Fern	145
Meeting the First Human Ancestors	148
Nature as a Healer	151
Creating a Dream Hoop	155
Inviting In the Ancestors	156
Preparation for Ceremony	159
Ceremony of Release and Surrender	160
Connecting with Water Element	162
Journeying with Orca	165
Merging with Lotus	166
Honouring the Precious	167
Setting Up Future Time Travel	168
Lotus Cleansing for Yourself	172
Lotus Cleansing for the Collective	173
Journeying to Python	175
Connecting to the Mythical through Nature	175
Setting Up Your Oracle Space	176
Unity Chant	178
Cord Making	179
Creating a DNA Python	179
Feeling the Serpent Power	181

Bibliography

Boring, F. M., Sloan, K. E., & Cheney, J. *Returning to Membership in Earth Community: Systemic Constellations with Nature*. Pagosa Springs, CO: Stream of Experience Productions, 2013.

Davis, R. *The Power to Be You*. Kentucky: Posidigm Press, 2018.

Gibran, K. and Butler-Bowdon, T. *The Prophet*. Newark, NJ, John Wiley & Sons Inc., 1923/2020.

Gilbert, E. *Big Magic: Creative Living beyond Fear*. New York: Riverhead Books, 2015.

Ingerman, S. *Medicine for the Earth: How to Transform Personal and Environmental Toxins*. New York: Random House International, 2001.

Kampenhout, D. *The Tears of the Ancestors: Victims and Perpetrators in the Tribal Soul*. Phoenix, AZ: Zeig, Tucker, and Theisen, 2008.

Kharitidi, O. *Entering the Circle: Ancient Secrets of Siberian Wisdom Discovered by a Russian Psychiatrist*. London: Thorsons, 1999.

Kimmerer, R. W. *Braiding Sweetgrass*. Old Saybrook, Ct: Tantor Media, Inc., 2021.

Macy, J., & Brown, M. Y. *Coming Back to Life: Practices to Reconnect Our Lives, Our World*. Gabriola Island, BC, Canada: New Society Publishers, 2014.

Moss, N. and Corbin, D. *Weather Shamanism*. Rochester, VT: Inner Traditions, 2008.

Perls, F. S., Goodman, P. and Hefferline, R.F. *Gestalt Therapy*. London: Souvenir Press, 2013.

Redmond, L. *When the Drummers Were Women: A Spiritual History of Rhythm*. New York: Three Rivers Press, 1997.

Acknowledgements

I have the small village of Dollar, the Ochil Hills, a room in the eaves of the bothy I lived in back then and two challenging lockdowns to thank for this book being produced. Out of the most testing times can a vision be born! So much gratitude, gorgeous Dollar, with special thanks to your Back Lane, the beech and oak tree glade by Quarrel Burn and the deli on Bridge Street for your godsend oat-milk takeaway cappuccinos on many a writer's-block morn.

I also acknowledge the ancestors of the land there, who came through in my morning space-opening and guided me to the portal sites. To the plants, trees, fae and birds for your communication and presence and to those incredible north winds who blew through so much magic and inspiration, I honour and thank you.

Gratitude to those who travelled with me through the writing and trying out of this material: Gillian Duncan; Emma Lees; Sarah Hulme; Nicola Anastasi; Emma Cowan; Karen Caddell Walker; Stefanie Harms; Anyta Lodge; Barbara Dawson; Claire Cathcart; Ally Button; Lavanya Balasubramanian; Zoé Poujade and Daniela Meier. Gratitude to you, dear reader, all through this book, for the vision for life that you weave with us.

I acknowledge Venus and north node in Taurus, as I am led by the message of this peaceful buffalo archetype. You have been carrying the vision for Earth since the time of the first ancestors I am sure; their drums and cave paintings show you there too! Thank you for appearing for me in this lifetime and for guiding this project.

Thank you to everyone who has worked with me over the years. You each hold a wonderful piece of a jigsaw of whose incredible design I am just beginning to get the impression.

I appreciate my supervision group of 2020 for holding space for me. I also hold in esteem my personal supervisor Liz Gentles for your steady holding and sense of humour. Honouring also Grant Clifford and the nurturing and support you provided as my supervisor for all those years.

I express heartfelt thanks to Sandra Ingerman. I cannot think of anyone more perfect to write the foreword for this book. You are a pioneer who brought this work into a Western world that wasn't yet conditioned to open to it and you just kept on going. I am so grateful for what has opened because of you, for your vision and for your friendship.

About the Author

Carol Day is an international visionary teacher, artist/film-maker and author. She lives in Scotland, UK, where she directs Creative Earth Ensemble, an innovative arts project. The creator of several nature-led models, her work brings great effectiveness for students, clients, organizations, and readers.

With an MFA in Fine Art in Context and an MSc in Counselling, Carol contributes to contemporary research. As a psychotherapist, constellation facilitator, and shamanic operator, she runs a successful private practice in Systemic Story Therapy.

In 2000, she was one of Scotland's chosen artists for the Year of the Artist. In 2007, she co-designed the Nature as Teacher model for Scotland's first outdoor nursery, which has won several awards. Commissioned to generate groundbreaking visionary story programmes working with inclusive community ethos and land, she was the presenter of the 2020 film *The River Tatha*.

For more information see: **www.creativeearthensemble.com**

FINDHORN PRESS

Life-Changing Books

Learn more about us and our books at
www.findhornpress.com

For information on the Findhorn Foundation:
www.findhorn.org